iOS 18.2 Bible

A Comprehensive and Simplified A-Z Guide for New Users and Seniors

Maxton C. K. Adams

iOS 18.2 Bible

Copyright © 2024 by Maxton C. K. Adams

All Rights Reserved.

No part of this book may be used or reproduced by any means, graphic, electronic, or mechanical, including photocopying, recording, taping, or by any information storage retrieval system without the written permission of the publisher.

iOS 18.2 Bible

TABLE OF CONTENTS

Introduction to iOS 18.2... 10
    What is iOS?... 10
    Overview of iOS 18.2 Features................... 12
        1. Refined User Interface...................... 12
        2. Smart AI Integration......................... 13
        3. Health and Wellness......................... 13
        4. Improved Messaging and Communication...................................... 13
        5. Advanced Camera and Photo Editing... 14
        6. Enhanced Privacy and Security........ 14
        7. Performance and Battery Life........... 15
        8. Augmented Reality (AR) and Gaming... 15
    Devices Compatible with iOS 18.2.............. 16
        iPhones... 16
        iPads... 17
        iPod Touch.. 17

Getting Started... 18
    Setting Up Your Device for the First Time... 18
    Understanding the Home Screen and Dock... 22

Apple ID and iCloud Essentials................... 25
Navigating iOS 18.2..................................... 29
    Using Touch Gestures and the Virtual
    Keyboard..29
        Common Touch Gestures..................... 30
        Using the Virtual Keyboard................... 32
    Control Center, Notifications, and Widgets. 34
        Control Center..35
        Notifications... 36
        Widgets... 38
    Spotlight Search: Finding Anything on Your
    Device..40
Customization and Personalization........................ 44
    Changing Wallpapers and Themes.............44
        Changing Your Wallpaper..................... 45
        Customizing Themes............................ 47
    Customizing the Control Center...................50
        Accessing and Customizing the Control
        Center.. 50
        Custom Controls for Quick Access....... 51
    Accessibility Features for Seniors...............52
        Vision and Display Settings................... 53
        Hearing Accessibility..............................54
        Motor Skills and Touch Accessibility..... 56
Communication Made Easy..58
    Making and Receiving Calls........................58
        Making a Call.. 59
        Receiving a Call..................................... 61
    Sending Texts and iMessages.................... 63

iOS 18.2 Bible

       Sending a Text Message (SMS)........... 63

       Using iMessage for Enhanced Features... 66

       Using FaceTime for Video and Audio Calls 68

       Making a FaceTime Video Call............. 69

       Making a FaceTime Audio Call............ 70

       FaceTime Across Devices.................... 71

Staying Organized..73

    Managing Contacts..73

       Creating and Managing Contacts......... 74

       Syncing Contacts with Other Apps....... 76

    Using the Calendar and Reminders Apps...78

       Using the Calendar App........................78

       Using the Reminders App..................... 81

    Notes and Voice Memos: Tools for Productivity.. 84

       Using the Notes App............................. 84

       Using the Voice Memos App.................86

Entertainment and Media..88

    Apple Music and Podcasts: Listening on iOS. 90

       Apple Music: Discover, Listen, and Share Music..90

       Podcasts: Stay Informed and Entertained 94

    Watching Videos on Apple TV and YouTube.. 96

       Apple TV: Movies, Shows, and Streaming Content... 97

       YouTube: The World's Largest Video

Platform 100
Taking and Editing Photos and Videos 102
    Taking Photos and Videos 102
    Editing Photos and Videos 104

Exploring the App Store 105
Searching for and Downloading Apps 106
    Getting Started with the App Store 107
    Using the Search Feature 108
    Downloading and Installing Apps 109
Managing App Updates and Subscriptions 111
    App Updates 112
    Managing Subscriptions 113
Essential Apps for Beginners 115
    Productivity and Organization Apps 115
    Entertainment Apps 117
    Social and Communication Apps 119
    Health and Fitness Apps 120

Staying Connected Online 121
Setting Up Wi-Fi and Mobile Networks 122
    Setting Up Wi-Fi 123
    Setting Up Mobile Networks 125
Using Safari for Browsing the Web 127
    Basic Browsing with Safari 127
    Advanced Safari Features 130
Managing Email Accounts with Mail 132
    Setting Up Email Accounts 133
    Composing, Sending, and Organizing Emails 135

Health and Fitness with iOS.................................**136**
    Setting Up the Health App........................ 138
        Getting Started with the Health App....139
    Tracking Steps, Workouts, and Medications... 142
        Tracking Steps and Daily Activity........142
        Tracking Medications............................ 145
    Using Emergency SOS and Medical ID....147
        Setting Up Emergency SOS............... 147
        Setting Up Medical ID......................... 149

Security and Privacy with iOS................................**151**
    Setting Up Face ID, Touch ID, or Passcodes.. 152
        Face ID.. 153
        Touch ID...155
        Passcodes... 157
    Managing App Permissions...................... 159
        Viewing and Managing App Permissions.. 159
    Using Private Relay and Hide My Email... 162
        Private Relay..163
        Hide My Email.................................... 165

Troubleshooting and Maintenance with iOS..........**166**
    Restarting, Updating, and Resetting Your Device.. 168
        Restarting Your Device....................... 169
        Updating Your Device......................... 170
        Resetting Your Device.........................172
    Managing Storage and Backups with iCloud..

174
    Managing Storage on iOS...................174
    Using iCloud for Backups....................176
Common Issues and How to Fix Them.....178
    1. iPhone Not Turning On................... 178
    2. Apps Freezing or Crashing............. 179
    3. Wi-Fi or Bluetooth Connectivity Issues. 180
    4. Battery Draining Quickly................. 181
    5. Slow Performance...........................182

Advanced Tips and Tricks for iOS 18.2.................. 182
    Using Siri for Voice Commands and Automation..183
    1. Voice Commands with Siri.............. 184
    2. Siri for Automation: Siri Shortcuts... 185
    3. Siri and Personal Automation:........ 187
    Creating and Managing Shortcuts............ 188
    1. Finding Pre-made Shortcuts........... 189
    2. Customizing Shortcuts.................... 189
    3. Organizing Shortcuts...................... 190
    4. Using Shortcuts Widgets.................190
    Connecting to Other Apple Devices..........191
    1. Continuity and Handoff.................... 191
    2. Apple Watch and iPhone Integration..... 192
    3. Connecting to Apple TV.................. 193
    4. AirPods and iPhone........................ 194
    5. iCloud Integration Across Devices.. 194

iOS 18.2 Hidden Gems... 195

iOS 18.2 Bible

Discovering New Features in iOS 18.2..... 196
   1. Enhanced Widgets Customization.. 197
   2. Live Activities in More Apps............ 198
   3. Focus Mode Enhancements........... 199
   4. Advanced Security Features for Privacy... 200
   5. Enhanced CarPlay Experience....... 201

Tips for Power Users................................ 202
   1. Multitasking with Stage Manager (for iPad Pro)... 202
   2. Automating Tasks with Advanced Shortcuts... 203
   3. App Clips for Quick Interactions...... 204
   4. Command Center Customization.... 205
   5. Screen Time Customizations for Advanced Control................................ 206

Upcoming Features in Future Updates..... 206
   1. Enhanced Augmented Reality (AR) Capabilities.. 207
   2. Pro Mode for Power Users.............. 207
   3. Health and Fitness Expansion........ 208
   4. More Focused Smart Home Integration 208
   5. iCloud Improvements...................... 208

Appendices... 210
   Glossary of iOS Terms............................. 210
   Keyboard Shortcuts for iPad and iPhone.. 216
      General Shortcuts for iPhone and iPad.... 216
      Shortcuts for iPad with External Keyboard

.... 218
Text Shortcuts.................................... 219
Special iPad Shortcuts....................... 219
Resources for Learning More................... 220
   1. Apple Support Website................... 220
   2. Apple Community Forums.............. 221
   3. iOS User Guide................................ 221
   4. iOS 18.2 Release Notes................. 222
   5. YouTube Channels.......................... 222
   6. Online Courses and Tutorials.......... 223
   7. Books... 223

iOS 18.2 Bible

Introduction to iOS 18.2

The introduction to iOS 18.2 is designed to provide users—especially new users, seniors, and beginners—with a solid foundation for understanding Apple's mobile operating system.

What is iOS?

iOS (formerly known as iPhone OS) is Apple's proprietary mobile operating system, designed exclusively for its range of mobile devices, including the iPhone, iPad, and iPod Touch. First introduced in 2007 with the launch of the original iPhone, iOS has evolved into a robust platform known for its seamless integration with

Apple's ecosystem, intuitive user interface, and emphasis on privacy and security.

Key Characteristics of iOS:

- **User-Friendly Interface**: Known for its simplicity and ease of use, making it especially accessible for beginners and seniors.
- **Tightly Integrated Ecosystem**: Works seamlessly with other Apple devices like Macs, iPads, and Apple Watches, enabling features like Handoff, AirDrop, and Continuity.
- **Frequent Updates**: Apple releases regular updates to improve functionality, enhance security, and introduce new features.
- **Privacy First**: iOS emphasizes user privacy with features like App Tracking Transparency, Private Relay, and secure Face ID or Touch ID authentication.

Overview of iOS 18.2 Features

Apple's iOS 18.2 builds upon the strengths of its predecessors while introducing new features, refinements, and enhancements to improve user experience. Whether you're a new user or an experienced Apple enthusiast, these updates aim to make your device more powerful, secure, and user-friendly.

1. Refined User Interface

- **Dynamic Lock Screen Widgets**: Customize your lock screen with live widgets that display real-time information, such as weather, calendar events, or fitness data.
- **Enhanced Customization**: More options for wallpapers, themes, and icon layouts, allowing for deeper personalization.

2. Smart AI Integration

- **Siri Enhancements**: Smarter responses, improved conversational context, and offline functionality for basic tasks.

- **Adaptive Typing Suggestions**: AI-driven suggestions that learn your typing style to provide more accurate word predictions.

3. Health and Wellness

- **Medication and Mood Tracking**: Enhanced tools in the Health app to track medications and record mood changes, aimed at promoting mental well-being.
- **Sleep Insights**: More detailed sleep analysis with recommendations for improving your sleep quality.

4. Improved Messaging and Communication

- **Live Stickers in Messages**: Create animated stickers from your own photos or videos for fun, expressive communication.
- **Real-Time Collaboration**: Share files, notes, or presentations directly from Messages and work collaboratively in real-time.

5. Advanced Camera and Photo Editing

- **Auto-Framing in Photos**: Automatically centers subjects in photos and videos for perfect shots every time.
- **Enhanced Photo Organizer**: Improved tagging and search features to quickly find photos based on location, event, or face recognition.

6. Enhanced Privacy and Security

- **App Privacy Reports**: Provides detailed insights into how apps use your data, including location, photos, and microphone access.
- **Emergency SOS Updates**: Expanded functionality, including voice activation for emergency calls and auto-alerting trusted contacts.

7. Performance and Battery Life

- Optimized battery usage through intelligent resource allocation, extending the time between charges.

- Improved performance, especially on older devices, making iOS 18.2 faster and smoother.

8. Augmented Reality (AR) and Gaming

- New AR tools for immersive experiences in gaming, shopping, and education.
- Game Mode prioritizes system resources for enhanced gaming performance.

Devices Compatible with iOS 18.2

iOS 18.2 supports a wide range of Apple devices, ensuring users can enjoy the latest features without necessarily upgrading their hardware. However, some features may be limited to newer models due to hardware requirements.

Here's a list of devices compatible with iOS 18.2:

iPhones

- iPhone 15, iPhone 15 Plus, iPhone 15 Pro, iPhone 15 Pro Max
- iPhone 14, iPhone 14 Plus, iPhone 14 Pro, iPhone 14 Pro Max
- iPhone 13, iPhone 13 Mini, iPhone 13 Pro, iPhone 13 Pro Max
- iPhone 12, iPhone 12 Mini, iPhone 12 Pro, iPhone 12 Pro Max
- iPhone 11, iPhone 11 Pro, iPhone 11 Pro Max
- iPhone SE (2nd generation and later)

iPads

- iPad Pro (all models)
- iPad Air (3rd generation and later)
- iPad (6th generation and later)
- iPad Mini (5th generation and later)

iPod Touch

- iPod Touch (7th generation)

While iOS 18.2 introduces exciting new features, older devices may not support some of them due to hardware limitations. If you're unsure whether your device can run iOS 18.2 or want to learn how to update your software, the book will provide step-by-step guidance in later chapters.

Getting Started

This chapter is designed to help new users, seniors, and beginners set up their iOS 18.2 device, navigate its home screen and dock, and understand the importance of an Apple ID and iCloud. Whether you're using an iPhone or an iPad, these foundational steps will help you get started smoothly and confidently.

Setting Up Your Device for the First Time

When you power on your iOS device for the first time, you'll be guided through the setup process. Here's a detailed step-by-step guide to ensure your device is configured correctly.

1. **Turn On Your Device**

- Press and hold the power button until the Apple logo appears.
- Follow the on-screen prompts to select your preferred language and region.

2. **Connect to Wi-Fi**

- Choose a Wi-Fi network from the list and enter the password.
- Connecting to a network is essential for activating your device and downloading updates.

3. **Set Up Face ID or Touch ID**

- For enhanced security, you can set up biometric authentication:
  - **Face ID**: Uses facial recognition to unlock your device.
  - **Touch ID**: Uses your fingerprint for unlocking and purchases.
- Follow the prompts to scan your face or fingerprint.

4. **Create a Passcode**

    - A six-digit passcode is required as a backup to biometric security.
    - You can choose a custom alphanumeric passcode for extra security.

5. **Sign In with Your Apple ID**

    - Enter your Apple ID email and password. If you don't have an Apple ID, you can create one during setup.
    - Your Apple ID is crucial for accessing Apple services like the App Store, iCloud, and Apple Music.

6. **Restore or Set Up as New**

    - Choose how you want to set up your device:
        - **Restore from iCloud Backup**: If you've used an Apple device before.

- **Restore from Mac/PC Backup**: If you have a backup saved on your computer.
- **Set Up as New Device**: For first-time users or fresh starts.

7. **Enable Siri and Services**

    o Configure Siri by speaking sample phrases.
    o Enable other features like Location Services, Apple Pay, and Screen Time as prompted.

8. **Update to the Latest iOS**

    o Check for and install any updates to ensure you have the latest features and security enhancements.

Once these steps are complete, your device is ready to use. Spend some time exploring the interface to become familiar with its layout and functionality.

Understanding the Home Screen and Dock

The home screen and dock are the central hubs of your iOS device, where you access apps, widgets, and settings. Here's a breakdown of their key components and how to use them effectively:

1. **The Home Screen**

    - **Apps**: Displays all installed apps in a grid layout. Tap any app icon to open it.
    - **Folders**: Group similar apps together by dragging one app over another. Name the folder to organize your screen.
    - **Widgets**: Interactive tiles providing quick access to information, like weather, calendar, or fitness data.
    - **Status Bar**: Located at the top, showing time, battery level, and network connection.
2. **Customization Tips**:

- Rearrange apps by long-pressing an icon until it jiggles, then drag it to your desired location.
- Use the App Library (swipe left past the last home screen) to find and organize apps efficiently.

3. **The Dock**

   - The dock is a persistent row of apps at the bottom of your screen.
   - By default, it includes frequently used apps like Messages, Safari, and Mail.
   - You can customize the dock by dragging apps in or out of this area.

4. **Pro Tips for Using the Dock**:

   - On iPads, the dock supports multitasking. Drag an app from the dock to open it in Split View or Slide Over mode.
   - Use the dock to quickly switch between recently used apps.

Understanding these features will help you navigate your device with ease and confidence.

Apple ID and iCloud Essentials

An Apple ID and iCloud account are the backbone of your iOS experience. They enable seamless access to Apple's ecosystem, allowing you to sync data, download apps, and safeguard your information.

1. **What is an Apple ID?**

    - Your Apple ID is a unique account used to log into all Apple services.
    - It's required for downloading apps, making purchases, and accessing iCloud, Apple Music, and more.
2. **Creating an Apple ID**:

    - Go to **Settings > Sign in to your iPhone** and follow the prompts.

- Provide your email address, create a password, and set up security questions.

3. **What is iCloud?**

    - iCloud is Apple's cloud storage service, designed to store your photos, documents, and backups securely.
    - It syncs data across all your Apple devices, ensuring you have access to your information anytime, anywhere.

4. **Key iCloud Features**:

    - **Photos**: Automatically uploads your pictures and videos to the cloud for safekeeping.
    - **iCloud Drive**: Stores documents and files that can be accessed from any device.
    - **Backup**: Automatically backs up your device, so you can restore it if something goes wrong.

- **Find My**: Helps you locate lost devices or share your location with trusted contacts.

5. **Setting Up iCloud**

    - Go to **Settings > Your Name > iCloud**.
    - Toggle the features you want to enable, such as Photos, Contacts, and Notes.
    - You receive 5GB of free iCloud storage. You can upgrade to a paid plan for more storage.

6. **Managing Your Apple ID**

    - Update your Apple ID settings by navigating to **Settings > Your Name**.
    - Change your password, update security questions, or manage your payment methods.
    - Turn on **Two-Factor Authentication** for extra security.

Why Are Apple ID and iCloud Important?

- They provide seamless access to Apple services and ensure your data is backed up and secure.
- With iCloud, you never have to worry about losing your data if you switch devices or encounter issues.
- They enable continuity features like Handoff, Universal Clipboard, and iCloud Keychain for a connected experience.

Navigating iOS 18.2

Navigating your iOS device is made easy thanks to the intuitive design of the interface. This section will cover the core methods of interacting with your device, including using touch gestures and the virtual keyboard, understanding the Control Center, managing notifications and widgets, and using Spotlight Search to find anything on your device. These tools will help you navigate iOS 18.2 with ease, whether you're a beginner, a senior user, or just looking to make the most of your device.

Using Touch Gestures and the Virtual Keyboard

One of the defining features of iOS devices is their reliance on touch gestures to interact with the operating system. Here's a breakdown of common gestures, as well as tips for using the virtual keyboard effectively.

Common Touch Gestures

1. **Tap**

    o Tap an app icon, button, or link to open or select it. A simple, quick touch activates most functions in iOS.
    o Tap and hold (also called a "long press") on an app or item to open additional options, such as moving or deleting apps.

2. **Swipe**

    o **Up Swipe**: Swipe from the bottom of the screen to open the **Control Center** (for quick settings) or the **App Switcher** (for managing apps you have open).
    o **Down Swipe**: Swipe down anywhere on the home screen to open **Spotlight Search** or swipe

down from the top-right corner to access **Notifications**.
- **Left/Right Swipe**: Swipe left or right on your home screen to switch between apps, screens, or panels. Swipe to the left on the lock screen to access widgets.

3. **Pinch and Zoom**

- **Pinch to Zoom In/Out**: This gesture is used in apps like Photos, Safari, Maps, and more to zoom in and out on images, text, or maps.
- **Spread with Two Fingers**: This gesture works similarly to pinch-to-zoom but is used for browsing larger content, such as zooming in on documents or photos.

4. **Drag**

- **Drag and Drop**: Press and hold an item, like an app icon or file, and move it to a new location. This works across different apps as well, like dragging a photo from Photos into a text message.

Using the Virtual Keyboard

The virtual keyboard is essential for typing on your iPhone or iPad. Here are some tips for using it efficiently:

1. **Typing on the Keyboard**

    - Tap individual keys to type. The keyboard will automatically adjust depending on the app you're using (e.g., a number pad in Calculator or an emoji keyboard in Messages).
    - **Shift and Caps Lock**: Tap the shift key for capital letters. Double-tap the shift key to activate Caps Lock.
    - **Special Characters**: Hold a key for alternative characters, such as pressing and holding the letter "E" for options like "é".

2. **Dictation**

    o Tap the microphone icon on the keyboard and speak your message or text. Siri's speech recognition will transcribe your speech into text in real-time.

3. **QuickPath (Swipe Typing)**

    o iOS supports swipe typing, allowing you to type words by swiping your finger across the keyboard, which can be faster than tapping each letter individually.

4. **Emoji and Symbols**

    o Tap the smiley face icon on the keyboard to access the emoji keyboard.
    o The globe icon switches between different language keyboards, so you can access emojis, symbols, and characters from other languages.

iOS 18.2 Bible

Control Center, Notifications, and Widgets

iOS 18.2 offers several ways to access key information quickly. The Control Center, Notifications, and Widgets make it easy to manage your device's settings and stay updated.

Control Center

The **Control Center** is a shortcut for accessing frequently used settings and tools, like Wi-Fi, Bluetooth, screen brightness, and volume control.

1. **Accessing Control Center**

    - On **iPhones with Face ID**, swipe down from the top-right corner of the screen.
    - On **iPhones with Touch ID**, swipe up from the bottom edge of the screen.
2. **Key Controls in the Control Center**

- **Wi-Fi and Bluetooth**: Tap to toggle these connections on/off.
- **Brightness and Volume**: Adjust screen brightness and device volume with sliders.
- **Airplane Mode**: Toggle airplane mode to disable wireless signals.
- **Focus Modes**: Quickly set up different Focus modes (e.g., Do Not Disturb, Personal, Work) to manage notifications and distractions.
- **Music and Media Controls**: Easily play, pause, and skip songs or videos, as well as adjust playback settings.
- **Screen Mirroring**: Cast your iOS device's display to a compatible screen like a TV or projector.
- **Alarm and Timer**: Set up timers or alarms directly from Control Center.

Notifications

Notifications allow you to stay updated on important messages, app alerts, and system messages.

1. **Accessing Notifications**

    - Swipe down from the top of the screen to reveal your **Notification Center**, which shows alerts from apps like Messages, Mail, and social media.
    - Notifications are sorted by time, with the most recent at the top.

2. **Managing Notifications**

    - Swipe left on any notification to **view**, **clear**, or **manage** it.
    - Tap on the notification to open the relevant app or view the message.
    - **Group Notifications**: iOS groups similar notifications together to reduce clutter. You can tap on a group to expand and view them all.

3. **Customizing Notifications**

    o Go to **Settings > Notifications** to adjust how notifications appear for each app. You can choose to have alerts displayed as banners, pop-ups, or in the Notification Center only.

Widgets

Widgets are mini-versions of apps that display information on your home screen or lock screen, providing quick access to relevant data.

1. **Adding and Customizing Widgets**

    o To add widgets to your home screen, long-press on an empty area of the screen and tap the + **icon** in the top-left corner.
    o Choose a widget from the list and drag it to your home screen or lock screen.

- Widgets can show data like weather, stock prices, calendar events, or news headlines.
- You can resize widgets by long-pressing and selecting the desired size.

2. **Interacting with Widgets**

- Tap on a widget to open the full app.
- Some widgets allow you to interact with them directly, such as marking a reminder as complete or checking the weather forecast.

3. **Smart Stack**

- The Smart Stack widget lets you cycle through multiple widgets in one spot. iOS intelligently switches between widgets based on your usage patterns (e.g., showing the weather in the morning and your calendar in the afternoon).

Spotlight Search: Finding Anything on Your Device

Spotlight Search is one of the most powerful tools in iOS 18.2, allowing you to search for apps, files, contacts, emails, and even information from the web, all from one place.

1. **Accessing Spotlight Search**

    - From the **Home Screen**, swipe down anywhere (except the top area where the status bar is).
    - Alternatively, swipe down from the **Lock Screen** to access Spotlight immediately without unlocking your device.

2. **Using Spotlight**

    - **Search for Apps**: Type the name of an app, and Spotlight will show it as a search result. Tap it to open the app.

- **Find Contacts**: Enter a contact's name to view phone numbers, emails, or messages.
- **Search for Files**: Enter the name of a document or note stored in the Files app to open it directly.
- **Look Up Web Content**: Spotlight searches the web through Siri Suggestions or Wikipedia and will display results from the web.
- **Quick Calculations and Conversions**: Type simple math problems or unit conversions (e.g., "5 miles in kilometers") directly into Spotlight to get instant answers.

3. **Refining Search Results**

- As you type, Spotlight will suggest potential results based on what you've typed. You can narrow down your search by tapping categories such as apps, documents, or emails.

4. **Siri Suggestions**

    o Spotlight Search is integrated with Siri Suggestions, which offers personalized search results based on your habits. If you frequently call a certain contact or open a particular app at specific times, Spotlight will show those suggestions.

Customization and Personalization

One of the strengths of iOS 18.2 is its ability to allow users to personalize and customize their devices to better suit their preferences and needs. From changing wallpapers and themes to customizing the Control Center, and even enabling accessibility features designed specifically for seniors, this chapter will guide you through the many ways you can make your device truly your own.

Changing Wallpapers and Themes

The look and feel of your iOS device can be significantly altered by changing its wallpaper and theme. These customizations are simple yet powerful ways to make your device feel more personalized.

Changing Your Wallpaper

The wallpaper is the background image that appears on your Lock Screen and Home Screen. iOS 18.2 allows for a high degree of personalization with both static and dynamic wallpapers, as well as custom photos.

1. **Setting a Wallpaper**

    - Go to **Settings > Wallpaper**.
    - Tap **Choose a New Wallpaper** to pick from Apple's built-in wallpaper options or use a photo from your library.
    - You can select from:
        - **Dynamic Wallpapers**: These move and change as you swipe or interact with your device.

- **Stills**: Static images that don't move.
- **Live Wallpapers**: These are interactive images that animate when you press the screen.
  - You can also choose to set different wallpapers for your **Lock Screen** and **Home Screen** for added flexibility.

2. **Personalizing Wallpaper**

   - If you prefer using your own photos, tap **All Photos** to browse your gallery.
   - Choose a photo and set it as your wallpaper by adjusting the size and positioning. You can pinch to zoom or move the photo to fit the screen.
   - Use the **Perspective Zoom** feature to add a dynamic effect where the wallpaper subtly moves as you tilt your device.

3. **Live and Lock Screen Customization**

    - For **Live Wallpapers**, tap and hold the Lock Screen to activate the animation, giving a dynamic and interactive touch to your Lock Screen experience.
    - You can create **photo-based wallpapers** by selecting favorite pictures or even set wallpapers based on special occasions (birthdays, holidays, etc.) with photos from your library.

Customizing Themes

Although iOS doesn't have full system-wide themes like some other operating systems, it does offer some level of customization through color schemes and accessibility settings.

1. **Dark Mode and Light Mode**

    - iOS supports **Dark Mode**, which changes the system-wide interface

- to a darker color scheme, reducing eye strain in low-light environments.
    - To enable it, go to **Settings > Display & Brightness** and choose between **Light** and **Dark**.
    - You can also schedule the appearance to switch automatically depending on the time of day.
2. **Accent Colors**
    - To adjust the overall theme to make it easier on the eyes, especially for seniors, you can use **Color Filters**. These filters change the colors of your entire device's interface.
    - To access this, go to **Settings > Accessibility > Display & Text Size > Color Filters**. Here, you can choose different color schemes such as grayscale, red/green filters, or blue/yellow to suit your visual preferences.

3. **Dynamic Wallpaper and Themes**

    o Combine **Dark Mode** with a dynamic wallpaper that shifts colors throughout the day for a more personalized aesthetic.
    o Use apps like **Shortcuts** to automate switching between themes or wallpapers based on time or location.

Customizing the Control Center

The **Control Center** is a powerful tool for quickly accessing essential settings and features on your device. iOS 18.2 allows you to customize which controls appear, making it more efficient for your needs.

Accessing and Customizing the Control Center

To open the Control Center:

- **iPhones with Face ID**: Swipe down from the top-right corner of the screen.
- **iPhones with Touch ID**: Swipe up from the bottom of the screen.

To customize what appears in the Control Center:

1. Go to **Settings > Control Center**.
2. You will see two sections: **Included Controls** (which are already in the Control Center) and **More Controls** (which you can add).
3. To add a control, tap the **green plus (+)** next to it in the "More Controls" section. For example, you can add shortcuts for **Screen Recording**, **Do Not Disturb**, **Flashlight**, or **Magnifier**.
4. To remove a control, tap the **red minus (-)** button next to it in the "Included Controls" section.
5. **Rearranging Controls**: You can reorder the controls by tapping and holding the three horizontal lines next to each control,

then dragging them to your preferred position.

Custom Controls for Quick Access

The more customized your Control Center, the easier it becomes to access the functions you use most. For instance:

- **Music Controls**: Add quick access for controlling media playback.
- **HomeKit Controls**: Add smart home device controls (like lights or thermostats) if you use HomeKit devices.
- **Screen Recording and Focus Modes**: Quickly toggle between focus settings such as **Do Not Disturb**, **Sleep**, or **Personal**.

By tailoring the Control Center to your habits and needs, you can save time navigating and accessing key features without needing to dig through settings.

Accessibility Features for Seniors

iOS is designed to be accessible for people of all ages, including seniors or those with visual, hearing, or motor impairments. iOS 18.2 offers a rich array of **accessibility features** that can be tailored for ease of use.

Vision and Display Settings

1. **Display Adjustments**

    - **Bold Text**: To make text easier to read, go to **Settings > Accessibility > Display & Text Size** and turn on **Bold Text**.
    - **Increase Contrast**: Increase contrast between text and background to make the text stand out better. Go to **Settings > Accessibility > Display & Text Size > Increase Contrast**.
    - **Text Size and Button Size**: Adjust the text and button sizes to suit your comfort by going to **Settings >**

Accessibility > Display & Text Size > Larger Text.
- **Zoom**: Enable the **Zoom** feature to magnify the content on your screen by double-tapping with three fingers. Go to **Settings > Accessibility > Zoom**.

2. **VoiceOver**

- VoiceOver is a powerful screen reader that reads out loud everything on your screen, making it ideal for seniors with visual impairments. To enable VoiceOver, go to **Settings > Accessibility > VoiceOver**, and turn it on.
- VoiceOver provides spoken descriptions of everything you touch, and users can navigate their device through gestures and commands.

Hearing Accessibility

1. **Live Listen**

    o With **Live Listen**, you can use your iPhone or iPad as a microphone to amplify sound for hearing aids or AirPods. Go to **Settings > Accessibility > Hearing Devices** to set it up.

2. **Sound Recognition**

    o iOS can recognize certain sounds (like a doorbell, a baby crying, or a dog barking) and alert you with a notification. To activate, go to **Settings > Accessibility > Sound Recognition** and toggle it on.

3. **Mono Audio**

    o For seniors with hearing impairments or those who prefer to hear sound through both ears equally, you can enable **Mono Audio**. This feature combines stereo channels into one. Go to

Settings > Accessibility > Audio/Visual > Mono Audio.

Motor Skills and Touch Accessibility

1. **AssistiveTouch**
   - **AssistiveTouch** helps users who have difficulty with physical touch or motor skills by providing an on-screen menu with custom gestures. It can simulate gestures like pinch, swipe, or tap, and also allows you to use shortcuts for hardware buttons. To enable, go to **Settings > Accessibility > Touch > AssistiveTouch**.
2. **Touch Accommodations**
   - **Touch Accommodations** can help users adjust the touch sensitivity of their device. For instance, you can slow down the touch response time or enable a hold feature to make it easier to perform certain actions. This can be found in **Settings >**

Accessibility > Touch > Touch Accommodations.

Communication Made Easy

Communication is one of the most important functions of a mobile device, and iOS 18.2 excels in providing easy, efficient, and versatile ways to stay connected with others. Whether it's making phone calls, sending text messages, or having video and audio calls, iOS 18.2 offers a range of features that make communication seamless.

Making and Receiving Calls

One of the fundamental features of any mobile device is the ability to make and receive phone calls, and iOS provides an intuitive and user-friendly experience for both tasks. Whether you're calling a contact, a business, or using features like FaceTime or Wi-Fi calling, iOS makes it easy to communicate via voice.

Making a Call

1. **Using the Phone App**

    - The **Phone app** is your primary tool for making calls. To access it, tap the **Phone** icon on your home screen.
    - **Dialing a Number**: On the main screen of the Phone app, tap the **Keypad** tab, and manually dial a phone number using the on-screen dial pad. Once you've entered the number, tap the **green call button** to initiate the call.
    - **Calling Contacts**: Tap the **Contacts** tab to scroll through your saved contacts. Tap a contact's name to see their phone number(s),

and then tap the **green call button** to place the call.
- **Call Using Siri**: You can ask Siri to call a contact by saying, "Hey Siri, call [contact name]." Siri will automatically place the call for you.

2. **Using Recent Calls**

   - The **Recents** tab in the Phone app displays your recent calls, both incoming and outgoing. To redial a number from this list, simply tap the **blue button** next to the contact or number.

3. **Making Calls with FaceTime**

   - In addition to traditional phone calls, iOS 18.2 allows you to make calls using **FaceTime** for both audio and video calls. This can be initiated either from the FaceTime app or directly from the Contacts app.

Receiving a Call

When you receive an incoming call, iOS offers several options for managing it:

1. **Answering or Rejecting a Call**

    - If your phone is locked, you'll see an incoming call notification on the **Lock Screen**. Tap **Accept** to answer the call or **Decline** to reject it.
    - If your phone is unlocked, you'll see the call appear as a notification, and you can either tap **Answer** or **Decline**.
2. **Silencing Calls**

    - You can mute the ringer by pressing the **side button** on the iPhone. This doesn't reject the call but will silence it.
    - You can also swipe the notification to send it directly to voicemail,

especially if you are busy or don't recognize the number.

3. **Blocking Unwanted Calls**

    o If you frequently receive calls from a certain number or spam calls, you can block the number in the **Phone app**. After receiving a call, tap the **i icon** next to the number, scroll down, and select **Block this Caller**.

4. **Wi-Fi Calling**

    o If you're in an area with poor cellular signal but have a strong Wi-Fi connection, you can enable **Wi-Fi calling**. This allows you to make and receive calls over Wi-Fi instead of cellular data. To enable this, go to **Settings > Phone > Wi-Fi Calling**, and toggle it on.

Sending Texts and iMessages

Text messaging is an integral part of modern communication, and iOS makes sending and receiving texts easy and efficient. The **Messages app** on iOS 18.2 supports not only traditional SMS text messaging but also **iMessages**, which are sent over the internet and offer enhanced features.

Sending a Text Message (SMS)

1. **Using the Messages App**

    - Tap the **Messages** app on your home screen to open it.
    - Tap the **compose button** (the pencil in a square) in the top-right corner to start a new message.
    - In the **To** field, enter the phone number or name of the recipient (if they are in your contacts).
    - Type your message in the text field at the bottom of the screen and tap the **send button** (blue or green arrow) to send the message.

2. **SMS vs. iMessage**

    - If your recipient is also using an iPhone and has **iMessage** enabled, your message will be sent as an **iMessage** (indicated by a blue bubble).
    - If they are not using an iPhone or do not have iMessage enabled, your message will be sent as a standard **SMS text message** (indicated by a green bubble).
    - iMessages are free and sent over the internet, while SMS messages are sent over the cellular network and may incur carrier charges.

3. **Sending Pictures, Videos, and Files**

    - Tap the **camera icon** next to the text input field to take a photo or video directly in the Messages app. You can also tap the **Photos icon** to choose an existing photo or video from your gallery.

- You can also attach documents, voice memos, and contact cards by tapping the **app icon** next to the input field.

Using iMessage for Enhanced Features

1. **Sending Text Effects and Stickers**

    - With **iMessage**, you can send animated text effects or stickers in your messages. After typing your message, press and hold the **send button** to choose between **Bubble Effects** (like "slam" or "loud") and **Screen Effects** (like fireworks or confetti).
    - You can also add stickers or emoji by tapping the **App Store icon** next to the text field, where you can download new stickers and apps for even more customization.

2. **Sending and Receiving Messages on Multiple Devices**

- With iCloud synchronization, your iMessages will sync across all your Apple devices. If you use an iPad, Mac, or Apple Watch, you can send and receive messages from those devices as long as you're logged into the same Apple ID.

3. **Group Chats and Mentions**

    - You can send messages to multiple people at once by creating a **group chat**. Group messages allow for collaborative conversations, and in iOS 18.2, you can also use **mentions** to get someone's attention in a busy group chat by typing their name preceded by the @ symbol (e.g., @John).

4. **Read Receipts and Typing Indicators**

    - iMessage allows you to see when a recipient has read your message (read receipts) and when they are typing a response. You can toggle

Read Receipts on or off by going to **Settings > Messages > Send Read Receipts**.
- Additionally, iMessage shows a **typing bubble** when the other person is writing a message.

Using FaceTime for Video and Audio Calls

FaceTime is a built-in app on iOS that allows you to make both **video calls** and **audio calls** to other Apple users. It's a fantastic tool for those who want to stay connected visually or need a reliable voice call service.

Making a FaceTime Video Call

1. **Using the FaceTime App**

    - Open the **FaceTime app**, tap the **plus (+) icon**, and enter the name, phone number, or email address of the person you want to call.

- Tap the **video camera icon** to initiate a video call.

2. **Using the Contacts or Phone App**

    - You can initiate a FaceTime call directly from your **Contacts** app or the **Phone app**. From the contact's page, tap the **FaceTime** button (video camera icon) to begin a video call.

3. **Switching Between Front and Rear Cameras**

    - During the FaceTime video call, you can tap the **camera icon** to switch between the front and rear cameras. This is useful if you want to show something around you during the conversation.

4. **Using FaceTime with Multiple People**

    - iOS 18.2 supports **Group FaceTime**, allowing up to 32 participants to join a video call simultaneously. Tap the **add participant** button during a call to invite more people. Each person's video feed will appear in a grid, and you can switch between different views.

Making a FaceTime Audio Call

1. **Initiating FaceTime Audio**

     - Open the **FaceTime app**, tap the **plus (+) icon**, and enter the contact details of the person you wish to call.
     - Tap the **phone icon** to initiate an **audio-only** call, which uses your Wi-Fi or cellular data instead of your regular phone service.

2. **Using FaceTime Audio from the Contacts or Phone App**

     - You can also initiate an audio-only FaceTime call directly from your

Contacts or **Phone app** by tapping the **FaceTime audio icon**.

FaceTime Across Devices

1. **Using FaceTime on iPad, Mac, or Apple Watch**
   - FaceTime calls can be answered or made from any Apple device that supports the app, as long as you are signed into the same Apple ID. If you're using an iPad or Mac, the interface is similar, but with a larger screen and additional controls for managing the call.
2. **Continuity for Seamless Communication**
   - With the **Continuity** feature, FaceTime calls can seamlessly transfer from one device to another. For example, if you start a call on your iPhone and then move to your Mac or iPad, the call can be picked up where you left off.

iOS 18.2 Bible

Staying Organized

One of the key benefits of iOS 18.2 is its ability to help users stay organized, whether managing contacts, scheduling events, setting reminders, or keeping track of thoughts and ideas. iOS provides a variety of apps designed to make life easier and more organized, all with intuitive interfaces and powerful features.

Managing Contacts

Your iPhone serves as a central hub for organizing and accessing the important people in your life. iOS 18.2 provides a well-integrated **Contacts app** that ensures you can easily store and retrieve phone numbers, email addresses, and other relevant details. You can also link contacts to your other apps for enhanced communication and productivity.

Creating and Managing Contacts

1. **Adding a New Contact**

    - Open the **Contacts** app and tap the **plus (+)** icon in the top-right corner to add a new contact.
    - Fill in the contact's details, such as name, phone number, email, address, and any other relevant information. You can also assign a profile picture by tapping **Add Photo**.

2. **Editing a Contact**

    - To edit an existing contact, open the **Contacts** app and search for the contact you wish to update. Tap the contact's name, then tap **Edit** in the top-right corner. Make your changes and tap **Done** to save.

3. **Linking Contacts**

    o iOS allows you to link contacts that may appear in multiple places. For instance, if someone has multiple phone numbers or email addresses, you can link them together under one contact. Tap **Edit** on a contact, scroll down to find the **Link Contacts** option, and select the contacts you want to combine.

4. **Using Siri to Add Contacts**

    o You can quickly add a new contact or update an existing one by using **Siri**. Just say, "Hey Siri, add a new contact" or "Hey Siri, update [contact name]'s phone number to [new number]."

5. **Managing Contact Groups**

    o You can organize your contacts into groups (e.g., Family, Friends, Work) using iCloud or third-party apps like **Groups**. Grouped contacts can make it easier to send bulk messages or manage specific subsets of your contacts.

6. **Contact Sharing**

    o iOS makes it simple to share contact information with others. To do this, open a contact's profile, tap **Share Contact**, and select how you'd like to share the details, whether through iMessage, email, or AirDrop.

Syncing Contacts with Other Apps

1. **iCloud**

    o By default, your contacts are synced with **iCloud**, ensuring they are available across all your Apple devices. To check or enable iCloud sync, go to **Settings > [Your Name] > iCloud**, and toggle on **Contacts**.

2. **Third-Party Apps**

    o iOS allows you to sync your contacts with third-party services like **Google Contacts** and **Microsoft Exchange**. Go to **Settings > Contacts > Accounts**, select the service, and toggle on **Contacts**.

3. **Merge Duplicate Contacts**

    o iOS can help you eliminate duplicate contacts in your list. To do this, go to **Contacts > Groups**, and tap **Find Duplicates**. iOS will automatically merge any matching entries.

Using the Calendar and Reminders Apps

The **Calendar** and **Reminders** apps in iOS 18.2 are excellent tools for managing your schedule, tasks, and reminders. These apps are tightly

iOS 18.2 Bible

integrated, so you can stay organized by keeping track of your events and to-dos in a single, easy-to-use interface.

Using the Calendar App

1. **Creating Events**

    o Open the **Calendar** app and tap the **plus (+)** icon in the top-right corner to create a new event.
    o Enter event details, including the event title, location, start and end times, and an optional description. You can also set **alerts** to remind you of the event, such as 10 minutes before or a day in advance.
    o If the event is recurring (e.g., weekly meetings), tap on **Repeat** to set the frequency.

2. **Viewing Your Calendar**

    o The Calendar app allows you to view your events in **Day, Week, Month**, or **Year** views. Use the

arrows in the top corners to navigate between dates.
- In the **Month view**, you can see the overview of events by tapping on specific days to view more details.

3. **Managing Events with Siri**

   - Siri can be a great assistant for scheduling events. Simply say, "Hey Siri, schedule a meeting at 3 PM tomorrow," and Siri will create the event for you.

4. **Sharing and Collaborating on Events**

   - You can invite others to events directly through the Calendar app. When creating or editing an event, tap **Add Invitees**, and enter the emails of the people you wish to invite.
   - This works well for team meetings or social gatherings, as all invited participants will receive a

notification and can respond to the event.
5. **Syncing with Other Calendars**

    o iOS supports integration with various third-party calendars, including **Google Calendar**, **Microsoft Outlook**, and **Exchange**. To sync these calendars, go to **Settings > Calendar > Accounts**, and add the relevant account.
    o You can choose which calendars to display and manage events from different services in one unified view.

Using the Reminders App

1. **Creating a Reminder**

    o The **Reminders app** is ideal for creating lists of tasks, shopping items, and personal reminders. To create a new reminder, open the app and tap **New Reminder**.

- Enter a title for your reminder, and then you can set a date, time, and location-based alert. For example, you can set a reminder to "Buy groceries" at 5 PM or when you arrive at a specific location like a store.

2. **Organizing Reminders with Lists**

    - You can organize reminders into different **lists** such as Personal, Work, or Shopping. Tap **Add List** at the bottom of the app to create a new list and then add your reminders to that specific list.
    - You can also use **tags** to categorize reminders and make them easier to search later. For example, you can tag reminders with labels like "Urgent," "Important," or "To Buy."

3. **Setting Priority and Due Dates**

- Reminders can be marked with different priority levels (low, medium, high) to indicate urgency. Tap the **i icon** next to a reminder to set the priority level.
- You can also set due dates and times for your reminders to ensure they get done on time. Notifications will alert you when the reminder is due.

4. **Collaborating on Reminders**

   - iOS allows you to share reminders with others and collaborate on lists. To share a list, tap **Edit**, select the list, and then tap **Share**. You can share your lists via iMessage or with others using iCloud.

5. **Using Siri with Reminders**

   - Siri can help you create reminders hands-free. Just say, "Hey Siri, remind me to call John at 3 PM," and Siri will add it to your Reminders app.

Notes and Voice Memos: Tools for Productivity

Both the **Notes** and **Voice Memos** apps are powerful tools for capturing ideas, jotting down important information, and staying organized throughout the day. Whether you're writing down thoughts, creating checklists, or recording memos, iOS has you covered.

Using the Notes App

1. **Creating and Organizing Notes**

    - Open the **Notes** app and tap the **create icon** (a square with a pencil) to begin writing a new note.
    - You can type text, insert photos, draw sketches, and even add checklists to keep your ideas organized. Notes can be formatted

with headings, bullet points, and numbered lists to make them clearer and easier to read.
2. **Organizing Notes into Folders**

    o Notes can be grouped into **folders** for better organization. Tap the **Back** button in the app to go to the main Notes screen, then tap **New Folder** at the bottom-left corner to create a new folder.
    o You can move notes into different folders by swiping left on a note, selecting **Move**, and choosing the appropriate folder.
3. **Sharing and Collaborating on Notes**

    o Similar to Reminders, you can share notes with others to collaborate on them. Tap the **Share** button at the top of a note, and select how you want to share it. You can even give other people permission to edit or view the note in real-time.

4. **Locking Notes**

    o If you want to keep sensitive information secure, you can **lock** notes with a password or Face ID/Touch ID. Open the note, tap the **Share** button, then tap **Lock Note**.
    o To unlock the note, you'll need to enter the password or authenticate with Face ID or Touch ID.

Using the Voice Memos App

1. **Recording Memos**

    o The **Voice Memos app** allows you to easily record audio notes, meetings, lectures, or ideas. Open the app, and tap

the **record button** (red circle) to start recording. Tap it again to stop.

- You can play back recordings, trim them, and rename them for easier identification.
2. **Organizing Recordings**

    o All your recordings are stored in the **Library** section of the Voice Memos app. You can tap **Edit** to rename or delete recordings, or swipe left on a memo to delete it.
3. **Sharing and Syncing Recordings**

    o You can share voice memos with others via AirDrop, email, or messages. Just tap the **Share** button on a recording and select your preferred method.

Entertainment and Media

One of the standout features of iOS 18.2 is its emphasis on entertainment and media, providing users with a wide range of options for enjoying music, podcasts, videos, and photography. Whether you're looking to unwind with your favorite playlist, catch up on podcasts, enjoy videos from streaming services like Apple TV and YouTube, or capture memories through photos and videos, iOS offers powerful tools and apps designed to enhance your media experience. In this section, we will explore how to use **Apple Music and Podcasts**, watch **videos on Apple TV and YouTube**, and make the most of **photos and video creation and editing** on your device.

Apple Music and Podcasts: Listening on iOS

iOS offers two prominent ways to enjoy audio entertainment: **Apple Music** for music streaming and **Podcasts** for audio content. Both apps are seamlessly integrated into the iOS ecosystem, offering an immersive and customizable experience.

Apple Music: Discover, Listen, and Share Music

1. **Getting Started with Apple Music**

    - Apple Music is a subscription-based streaming service that offers access to millions of songs, curated playlists, and exclusive content. To get started, open the **Apple Music** app, where you can subscribe to a plan (Individual, Family, or Student) if you haven't already.

- Apple Music offers a 3-month free trial for new users, giving you access to all features without restriction. Once you subscribe, you can stream music ad-free and download your favorite tracks for offline listening.

2. **Discovering Music**

   - The **For You** tab recommends playlists, albums, and songs based on your listening history and preferences. Apple Music's algorithm learns your musical taste over time, offering personalized suggestions.
   - In the **Browse** tab, you can explore curated playlists, top charts, genres, and new releases. Apple Music also highlights **new music**, **radio stations**, and **exclusive artist content**.

3. **Creating and Sharing Playlists**

- To create a playlist, tap **Library > Playlists > New Playlist**. You can add songs from your library or search for new music to add. Once your playlist is created, you can share it with friends via **iMessage**, **AirDrop**, or **social media** platforms.
- Apple Music also supports collaborative playlists, allowing you to invite friends to add and modify the playlist, making it perfect for social listening experiences.

4. **Listening Offline**

- Apple Music allows users to download their favorite tracks, albums, and playlists for offline listening. Tap the **download icon** next to a song or album to save it to your device for listening without an internet connection.

5. **Using Siri with Apple Music**

    o Siri integration allows you to control your music hands-free. You can say things like, "Hey Siri, play my workout playlist," or "Hey Siri, play the latest album by [artist name]," to start playing music without unlocking your device.

Podcasts: Stay Informed and Entertained

1. **Getting Started with Podcasts**

    o Open the **Podcasts** app on your iPhone to access a wide variety of audio content, ranging from news, comedy, storytelling, and education, to specialized content for all interests. Podcasts are typically available for free and can be streamed or downloaded for offline listening.
    o The app offers curated recommendations, including **Top**

Charts, **New Releases**, and **Trending Podcasts**.
2. **Subscribing and Managing Podcasts**

    o To listen to a podcast, tap on an episode and hit **play**. If you find a podcast you like, you can subscribe to it by tapping the **Subscribe** button. This will allow new episodes to automatically appear in your **Library**.
    o You can manage your subscriptions by going to **Library > Shows**, where you can easily navigate your podcasts and mark episodes as played or save them for later listening.

3. **Creating a Playlist**

    o You can create custom playlists of your favorite podcast episodes, much like music playlists, by selecting episodes and adding them to your **Library**. This can help you

stay organized if you regularly listen to multiple shows.
4. **Using Siri for Podcast Control**

    o Siri can also be used to control podcast playback. Say, "Hey Siri, play the latest episode of [Podcast Name]" or "Hey Siri, skip to the next episode," and Siri will handle it for you, making listening more convenient while multitasking.

Watching Videos on Apple TV and YouTube

iOS provides seamless access to video content, from movies and TV shows on **Apple TV** to videos, vlogs, and tutorials on **YouTube**. Both platforms offer a rich experience, with a few distinct features and content types for users to explore.

Apple TV: Movies, Shows, and Streaming Content

1. **Getting Started with Apple TV**

    - **Apple TV** is a platform that provides access to movies, TV shows, live sports, and more through various subscription services. With **Apple TV+**, Apple's own streaming service, users can enjoy exclusive original content such as series, movies, and documentaries.
    - You can download the **Apple TV app** on iOS devices, Smart TVs, and streaming boxes to access all your Apple TV content. If you're subscribed to Apple TV+, you can stream movies and shows directly within the app.

2. **Navigating Apple TV**

    - On the **Apple TV app**, the **Watch Now** section features personalized recommendations based on your previous viewing habits. Here you

can see new releases, trending content, and shows that you might like.
- In addition to Apple's original content, Apple TV integrates third-party services like **HBO Max**, **Netflix**, **Disney+**, and more, allowing you to watch videos from multiple platforms in one app.

3. **Renting or Buying Movies**

   - In the **Apple TV app**, you can rent or purchase movies from the **iTunes Store**. These movies are available for download or streaming and often come in HD or 4K resolution.

4. **Using AirPlay to Stream to Other Devices**

   - With **AirPlay**, you can wirelessly stream video content from your iPhone to an **Apple TV** or any AirPlay-enabled smart TV. Simply tap the **AirPlay icon** in the video player to start streaming to another screen.

5. **Managing Subscriptions and Family Sharing**

    o You can manage your Apple TV+ subscription and share access with family members via **Family Sharing**. This feature allows up to six people in your family to enjoy Apple TV+ content using their own devices.

YouTube: The World's Largest Video Platform

1. **Accessing YouTube**

    o The **YouTube app** provides access to an endless array of videos, ranging from music videos, how-to tutorials, vlogs, and live streams, to documentaries and full-length movies. Open the YouTube app, tap the **Search icon**, and explore

content by keyword, trending topics, or channel.
2. **Subscribing to Channels**

    - You can subscribe to your favorite YouTube channels to get updates when new videos are posted. Just tap the **Subscribe** button on the channel's page to stay up to date with their latest content.
3. **Watching and Sharing Videos**

    - Watching videos on YouTube is simple. Tap any video to start streaming it. You can also adjust video quality, enable captions, or watch in full-screen mode.
    - You can share videos via iMessage, email, social media, or other apps directly from the YouTube app. Tap the **Share** button to send the video to others.
4. **YouTube Premium**

- **YouTube Premium** offers an ad-free experience, the ability to download videos for offline viewing, and access to **YouTube Music**, which is a great option for those who enjoy listening to music on YouTube without interruptions.

5. **AirPlay with YouTube**

    - Like with Apple TV, you can use **AirPlay** to stream YouTube videos to larger screens. Tap the **AirPlay icon** while watching a video, and select an AirPlay-enabled device to cast the video to a TV or speaker.

Taking and Editing Photos and Videos

The **Camera app** on iOS has long been a powerful tool for capturing high-quality images and videos. With iOS 18.2, the Camera app includes advanced features such as portrait mode, night mode, and cinematic video modes.

Additionally, iOS provides extensive editing tools for both photos and videos, making it a robust platform for content creation.

Taking Photos and Videos

1. **Using the Camera App**

     - Open the **Camera app** and swipe through the options for **Photo**, **Portrait**, **Video**, **Time-Lapse**, and **Slow-Mo**. You can also use the **Burst mode** (hold the shutter button) to take rapid shots in quick succession.
     - The iPhone 15 series includes **ProRAW** and **ProRes** for advanced photography and videography, allowing you to capture high-quality images and videos for professional editing.

2. **Using the Front and Rear Cameras**

     - The iPhone includes front and rear-facing cameras, both equipped

with different features for selfies and standard photography. Switch between them by tapping the **flip icon** in the Camera app.
3. **Adjusting Focus and Exposure**

    o Tap to set the focus on a particular subject, and slide the exposure control to adjust the brightness of your image.

Editing Photos and Videos

1. **Editing Photos**
    o Open the **Photos app**, select the photo you want to edit, and

tap **Edit**. iOS offers robust editing tools such as adjusting exposure, contrast, brightness, color filters, cropping, rotating, and red-eye correction.

- You can also use the **Markup** tool to add text, shapes, and draw on your photos.
2. **Editing Videos**

- iOS also offers video editing capabilities directly in the **Photos app**. You can trim video clips, adjust exposure, brightness, and contrast, apply filters, and even create slow-motion effects or time-lapse sequences.
- For more advanced video editing, you can use third-party apps like **iMovie**, which provides more creative control over video edits.

Exploring the App Store

The **App Store** is the central hub for discovering, downloading, and managing apps on iOS devices. With millions of apps available, it serves as a gateway to enhancing your device's capabilities, from productivity tools to entertainment, health, and social media apps. Whether you're a beginner or a seasoned user, understanding how to effectively explore, manage, and organize apps will make your iOS experience more enjoyable and efficient.

Searching for and Downloading Apps

The **App Store** is the primary place for finding apps that can meet your needs, whether for entertainment, work, or personal growth. The store is organized into categories, featuring a wide variety of apps for users of all types. Below, we'll dive into how you can find, download, and install apps on your iPhone.

Getting Started with the App Store

1. **Opening the App Store**

    - To access the **App Store**, tap the **App Store icon** on your home screen. The app opens to a variety of sections, including **Today**, **Games**, **Apps**, **Arcade**, and **Search**.
    - On the main page, you will see curated content, including top charts, featured apps, and new releases.

2. **Browsing for Apps**

- The **Today** tab highlights daily updates, app recommendations, and stories about apps, making it easy to discover new and popular apps.
- The **Apps** and **Games** tabs break down apps into subcategories, such as **Productivity**, **Lifestyle**, **Entertainment**, **Health & Fitness**, and **Education**.
- **Apple Arcade** offers a subscription-based service with access to hundreds of exclusive games for iOS devices.

Using the Search Feature

1. **Searching for Apps**

    - Tap the **Search** icon (magnifying glass) at the bottom of the App Store to enter search mode. Type keywords related to what you are looking for—whether it's a specific app name or a category (e.g., "fitness" or "photo editor").

- The search results will show you apps that match your query, sorted by relevance and popularity. You can filter the results by **Top Charts**, **Categories**, or **Recently Updated** to narrow down your choices.

2. **App Recommendations**

    - Based on your search history and preferences, the **App Store** also recommends apps that you might be interested in. These suggestions are shown in the search results or on the **Today** tab, making it easier to find apps related to your interests.

Downloading and Installing Apps

1. **Downloading Free Apps**

    - To download a free app, tap the app's listing in the search results or on a featured page. You will be taken to the app's page, where you can read more about it, check

reviews, view screenshots, and see its rating.
- Tap the **Get** button (or the cloud icon if you've downloaded the app before). You may be prompted to authenticate using **Face ID**, **Touch ID**, or your **Apple ID password**.
2. **Purchasing Paid Apps**

    - Paid apps are clearly marked with their price next to the **Get** button. To purchase a paid app, tap the price, then confirm your purchase using your chosen authentication method. Once the payment is processed, the app will begin downloading.
3. **Automatic Downloads**

    - You can enable **Automatic Downloads** for apps to be downloaded on all your devices. To enable this feature, go to **Settings > [Your Name] > iTunes & App**

Store, and toggle on **Apps** under the Automatic Downloads section.

Managing App Updates and Subscriptions

After downloading apps, it's important to keep them up-to-date for new features, bug fixes, and security improvements. Additionally, many apps offer subscriptions for premium content, and managing these is crucial for avoiding unnecessary charges.

App Updates

1. **Checking for Updates**

   - Open the **App Store**, then tap your **profile icon** in the top-right corner. Here, you will see a list of available updates for apps that you have installed. You can update individual apps by tapping **Update** next to the app or tap **Update All** to update all apps at once.

2. **Enabling Automatic App Updates**

    o To avoid manually updating apps, enable automatic updates by going to **Settings > [Your Name] > iTunes & App Store**, and toggle on **App Updates** under **Automatic Downloads**.

3. **What's New in Updates**

    o App updates often include release notes detailing new features, bug fixes, and enhancements. To see these notes, tap the app in the **App Store** and scroll down to the **Version History** section.

Managing Subscriptions

1. **Understanding Subscriptions**

    o Many apps offer subscriptions, such as premium versions, content services (e.g., streaming), or in-app purchases. Common examples

include **Apple Music, Apple TV+, Netflix**, and fitness apps.
- To view and manage your subscriptions, go to **Settings > [Your Name] > Subscriptions**. This section shows all active and expired subscriptions tied to your Apple ID.

2. **Renewing or Cancelling Subscriptions**

    - In the **Subscriptions** menu, you can tap on any app to see the details of your subscription. You can renew or cancel subscriptions directly from here.
    - If you cancel a subscription, you can continue to use it until the end of your current billing cycle, after which the service will no longer be available.

3. **Free Trials and Subscriptions**

    - Many services offer free trials. Be mindful of the trial's expiration date and how much you will be charged if you continue the subscription after the trial ends. You can manage the trial by following the same steps as for any subscription.

Essential Apps for Beginners

For new iOS users, there are several essential apps that can significantly improve the iPhone experience, whether for productivity, communication, or entertainment. While every user's preferences differ, here's a list of apps that are highly recommended for those just starting out.

Productivity and Organization Apps

1. **Notes**

    - The **Notes** app allows you to jot down ideas, create to-do lists, and organize your thoughts. It's simple but powerful, allowing you to add photos, links, checklists, and even sketches to your notes.

2. **Reminders**

    o This app is perfect for organizing tasks and setting reminders for important events. It's ideal for making shopping lists, managing work tasks, or remembering appointments.

3. **Calendar**

    o iOS's built-in **Calendar** app helps users organize their schedule. You can set reminders, repeat events, and sync with Google or other accounts, ensuring all your important dates are easy to track.

4. **Mail**

    o **Mail** is iOS's default email app. It supports multiple email accounts, including iCloud, Gmail, Yahoo, and Outlook, and offers tools like

sorting, flagging, and searching through your inbox.
5. **Safari**

    o **Safari** is the default browser for iOS, offering fast browsing, private mode, and synchronization with your iCloud bookmarks and tabs across devices. It's a vital tool for web browsing.

Entertainment Apps

1. **Apple Music**

    o As one of the best music streaming services, **Apple Music** offers access to millions of songs, curated playlists, and exclusive content. It's perfect for music lovers who want a seamless listening experience across all devices.

2. **Podcasts**

- The **Podcasts** app allows you to explore and listen to a wide range of podcasts on any topic. It's perfect for staying informed, entertained, and inspired during your commute or workout.

3. **YouTube**

    - YouTube is the go-to platform for watching videos, from music videos and tutorials to vlogs and documentaries. The **YouTube** app lets you access your subscriptions, playlists, and even stream live content.

Social and Communication Apps

1. **Messages**

    - **Messages** allows you to send text messages, pictures, voice notes, and videos. You can also send **iMessages** to other Apple users for free, as well as make group chats.

2. **FaceTime**

    - Use **FaceTime** to make video and audio calls to other Apple users. It's a secure and reliable way to stay connected with friends and family.

3. **WhatsApp**

    - **WhatsApp** is a popular third-party messaging app that allows users to send messages, make voice and video calls, and share photos and videos globally.

4. **Facebook and Instagram**

    - These two social media giants help you stay connected with friends and family. With **Facebook**, you can post updates, share photos, and interact with others. **Instagram** is all about sharing photos and stories and following visual content creators.

Health and Fitness Apps

1. **Health**

   - The **Health** app consolidates all your health data in one place. It tracks your steps, heart rate, and sleep patterns, and integrates with other fitness apps to give you a comprehensive overview of your wellness.

2. **Fitness**

   - The **Fitness** app provides access to **Apple Fitness+**, a subscription service offering guided workouts, meditation sessions, and more, tailored to your fitness goals.

Staying Connected Online

In today's world, staying connected online is essential for work, communication, entertainment, and information. iOS devices, including iPhones and iPads, offer a range of tools and features to ensure that users can easily set up internet connections, browse the web, and manage email accounts seamlessly. Whether you're at home, on the go, or at work, iOS makes staying connected online straightforward with powerful features like **Wi-Fi, mobile networks, Safari for web browsing**, and **Mail for email management**.

Setting Up Wi-Fi and Mobile Networks

Having a stable and fast internet connection is key to making the most of your iOS device. iOS devices offer flexible options for internet connectivity, whether via **Wi-Fi** at home or a **mobile data** plan on the go.

Setting Up Wi-Fi

1. **Connecting to a Wi-Fi Network**

    - To connect to a Wi-Fi network, open **Settings** and tap **Wi-Fi**. Ensure that Wi-Fi is turned on by toggling the switch to green.
    - Your device will automatically scan for available Wi-Fi networks nearby. Tap the name of the network you wish to join, and if it's secured, you'll be prompted to enter the network's password.
    - Once connected, you'll see a checkmark next to the Wi-Fi network name, indicating a successful connection. You can also

see the **Wi-Fi signal strength** in the status bar at the top of your device.

2. **Advanced Wi-Fi Settings**

    o If you need to troubleshoot a connection or change settings, tap on the **information icon (i)** next to the network name. Here, you can **forget** a network, disable **Auto-Join**, or adjust the **DNS settings**.
    o The **Auto-Join** feature automatically connects your device to known networks without prompting you. This is useful for home or office networks but can be turned off for public or less secure networks.

3. **Wi-Fi Calling**

    o If you're in an area with poor cellular signal but have access to Wi-Fi, you can enable **Wi-Fi Calling**. Go to **Settings > Phone >**

Wi-Fi Calling and toggle it on. This allows you to make and receive calls over Wi-Fi when cellular coverage is limited.

Setting Up Mobile Networks

1. **Turning on Mobile Data**

   o To enable **mobile data**, go to **Settings > Cellular**, and toggle on **Cellular Data**. This allows you to use mobile data for internet access when Wi-Fi is not available.

   o You can also enable **Data Roaming** for when you travel abroad, but be mindful of potential additional charges from your carrier.

2. **Managing Mobile Data Usage**

   o iOS lets you track your **data usage** so you can avoid exceeding your mobile data plan's limit. In **Settings > Cellular**, you can see how much data you've used in the current

period. You can reset these statistics at the beginning of each billing cycle.
- You can also disable **mobile data** for individual apps by scrolling down to the app list in **Settings > Cellular** and toggling off mobile data for apps that you don't need to access online.

3. **Choosing Between Wi-Fi and Mobile Data**

    - iOS automatically prioritizes **Wi-Fi** over **mobile data** when both are available, but you can disable Wi-Fi and rely on mobile data if needed. You can switch between the two connections by simply toggling the Wi-Fi switch in **Settings** or using the **Control Center** for quick access.

Using Safari for Browsing the Web

Safari is the default web browser on iOS devices and offers a fast, secure, and seamless browsing experience. With features like **private browsing**, **tabs**, and **syncing across devices**, Safari ensures you can stay connected to the internet effortlessly.

Basic Browsing with Safari

1. **Opening Safari**

    - To start browsing, tap the **Safari icon** on your home screen. The browser opens to a **Start Page** with options like **Frequent Sites**, **Siri Suggestions**, and **Reading List**. You can also access **bookmarks** and **history** from this screen.

2. **Searching the Web**

    - In the address bar, type in a website address (URL) to visit a specific page, or enter a search term to use the built-in search engine (Google, by default) to find information.

- Safari supports **Voice Search**—just tap the **microphone** icon in the search bar and speak your search query.

3. **Navigating Websites**

    - You can tap links to open new pages, swipe to go back and forward, and pinch to zoom in or out of text and images on a webpage.
    - Safari offers a **Reader View** for articles and blogs, which strips away ads, sidebars, and other distractions, leaving you with clean, readable content. To enable Reader View, tap the **Reader icon** (four lines) in the address bar.

4. **Using Tabs**

    - Safari allows you to open multiple web pages at once in **tabs**, similar to how browsers work on desktop computers. Tap the **Tabs icon** (two

overlapping squares) in the bottom-right corner to view all open tabs.
- You can open a new tab by tapping the + **icon**, and swipe left or right to switch between open tabs.

5. **Bookmarking and History**

- To save a webpage for easy access later, tap the **Share icon** (square with an upward arrow), then select **Add Bookmark**. You can access all your bookmarks in the **Bookmarks icon** (book symbol) on the Safari toolbar.
- You can also view your browsing history by tapping the **History icon** (clock symbol) to revisit previously viewed sites.

Advanced Safari Features

1. **Private Browsing**

- For browsing without saving your history, enable **Private Browsing**. Tap the **Tabs icon**, then tap **Private** to activate this mode. In this mode, Safari doesn't store browsing history, cookies, or cached data, making it ideal for temporary browsing.

2. **Safari Extensions**

    - iOS supports **Safari Extensions** to enhance the browsing experience. To explore extensions, go to **Settings > Safari > Extensions**, and browse through available options to install.

3. **Handoff**

    - If you're using Safari on multiple Apple devices, you can use **Handoff** to seamlessly switch from one device to another. For example, if you're browsing a webpage on your iPhone, you can pick up right

where you left off on your iPad or Mac.
   4. **Autofill and Passwords**
      o Safari can remember passwords for websites, making it easier for you to log in. Go to **Settings > Safari > Autofill** to enable features like autofill for contact info, passwords, and credit card details.

Managing Email Accounts with Mail

The **Mail** app is a powerful email client that allows you to manage multiple email accounts from various providers such as **iCloud**, **Gmail**, **Yahoo**, **Outlook**, and more. With its intuitive interface and deep integration into the iOS ecosystem, Mail makes it simple to stay on top of your email.

Setting Up Email Accounts

1. **Adding an Email Account**

    o To add a new email account, open **Settings > Mail > Accounts**, then tap **Add Account**. Select your email provider (e.g., iCloud, Gmail, Yahoo) or choose **Other** to manually add your account using your email address and password.
    o After adding the account, you can choose which features to sync with your device, such as **Mail**, **Contacts, Calendars**, and **Notes**.

2. **Switching Between Accounts**

    o The Mail app allows you to manage multiple email accounts in a unified inbox. In the **Mail app**, you can switch between accounts by tapping the **Mailbox** button in the upper-left corner. Here, you'll see a list of all your email accounts and can choose to view one or all of them.

3. **Managing Folders and Organizing Mail**

    - You can create custom folders for your emails within the **Mail app**. To create a folder, tap **Edit** in the Mailboxes view, then tap **New Mailbox** and give it a name.
    - Move emails to folders by swiping left on an email and selecting **Move**, then choosing the desired folder.

Composing, Sending, and Organizing Emails

1. **Composing an Email**

    - To compose a new email, tap the **Compose button** (pen and paper icon) in the lower-right corner of the Mail app. Enter the recipient's email address, subject line, and message, then tap **Send** when ready.
    - You can attach photos, documents, or other files by tapping the

attachment icon below the message body.
2. **Using Rich Text and Formatting**

    o When composing an email, tap the **Aa icon** to bring up rich text formatting options. You can change the font, size, and style, and add bold, italics, or underline to your text.
3. **Managing Email Threads**

    o iOS Mail automatically groups related emails into **threads** to keep conversations organized. You can swipe left to delete or archive emails and use the **Mark** option to flag important emails or mark them as read/unread.
4. **Search and Sorting**

    o The **Search bar** at the top of the Mail app lets you search through your emails by keyword, sender, or date. You can also sort emails by date, sender, or subject to quickly find what you need.

Health and Fitness with iOS

iOS devices, particularly iPhones and Apple Watches, offer a suite of powerful health and fitness tools designed to help users track their physical activity, monitor health metrics, and maintain a balanced lifestyle. Apple's **Health app** is the central hub for managing health-related data, offering seamless integration with the **Apple Watch** and third-party apps. Whether you're looking to track your steps, workouts, or medications, or use emergency features like **Emergency SOS** and **Medical ID**, iOS provides an extensive set of features to help users live healthier and stay safe.

Setting Up the Health App

The **Health app** is pre-installed on iOS devices, acting as the primary interface to track and store a variety of health-related information. Whether you want to monitor daily activity or set long-term fitness goals, the app makes it easy to consolidate data from different sources into one place.

Getting Started with the Health App

1. **Opening the Health App**

    - To start, tap the **Health app** icon on your device. The app opens to the **Summary** tab, where you can see an overview of your health and fitness metrics. This page gives you a snapshot of your activity, steps, sleep, heart rate, and more, all on a daily, weekly, or monthly basis.
2. **Setting Up Health Profiles**

- When you first open the app, you'll be prompted to enter some basic information to personalize your health profile. This includes your **age**, **sex**, **height**, **weight**, and **fitness level**. You can adjust this data at any time by going to **Health App > Profile**.
- This information is important as it helps to tailor health tracking to your specific needs, improving the accuracy of your fitness and health insights.

3. **Granting App Permissions**

    - Many third-party apps and devices (such as fitness trackers and smart scales) integrate with the Health app. When you first install these apps or connect devices, you'll be prompted to grant them access to your Health data. The Health app will ask you to allow or deny access to specific types of data, such as

steps, heart rate, workouts, and more.
4. **Health Data Categories**

    o The Health app organizes your health data into **categories** such as **Activity**, **Mindfulness**, **Body Measurements**, **Nutrition**, and **Sleep**. These categories help you see an overview of your wellness and make it easier to locate the metrics you're interested in.

5. **Syncing with Apple Watch**

    o If you own an **Apple Watch**, it integrates seamlessly with the Health app to provide more detailed tracking of workouts, heart rate, calories burned, and sleep patterns. Ensure your Apple Watch is connected to your iPhone by checking Bluetooth settings to sync health data between the two devices.

Tracking Steps, Workouts, and Medications

iOS devices, especially with the help of the **Apple Watch**, offer a variety of ways to track your activity, workouts, and medications. The **Health app** consolidates this data in real-time, allowing you to monitor your health progress and make adjustments when needed.

Tracking Steps and Daily Activity

1. **Step Tracking with the Health App**

    - iPhones, equipped with motion sensors, track your daily steps automatically. You can view this data in the **Health app** under the **Activity** category. The **Steps** section shows your step count for each day, along with weekly and monthly trends.
    - The **Activity** ring (also visible on Apple Watch) helps you monitor

your **move**, **exercise**, and **stand** goals. The **Move** goal tracks calories burned through activity, **Exercise** measures time spent exercising, and **Stand** shows how often you stand up and move around during the day.
- If you have an **Apple Watch**, it will more accurately track your steps and activity levels, syncing this data with the Health app in real-time.

2. **Monitoring Workouts**

- You can manually log workouts in the **Health app** or use the **Workout app** on the Apple Watch to automatically track a variety of exercises such as running, walking, cycling, yoga, swimming, and strength training.
- The **Workout app** records important metrics during workouts, such as **calories burned**, **heart rate**, **distance**, and **duration**,

depending on the activity type. These metrics are then synced with the Health app for easy tracking and analysis.

3. **Tracking Active Minutes and Calories**

    o In addition to tracking steps, iOS allows you to monitor your **active minutes** and calories burned during physical activities. If you use an Apple Watch, these metrics are more comprehensive and provide real-time feedback on your efforts, motivating you to stay active.

Tracking Medications

1. **Managing Medications in the Health App**

    o The Health app includes a built-in **Medications** feature that allows you to track your prescriptions, over-the-counter medications, and supplements. To start using this

feature, open the **Health app**, select the **Browse** tab, and tap **Medications**.
- You can add medications by tapping the **Add Medication** button, and then entering the medication's name, dose, and frequency. The app will remind you when it's time to take your medications based on the schedule you set.

2. **Setting Medication Reminders**

    - The Health app will send you reminders at the times you've scheduled for taking your medication, helping you stick to your prescribed regimen. You can track your progress and ensure that you're consistently taking your medications as prescribed.

3. **Medication List and History**

    - All medications, doses, and schedules are saved within the app, and you can view your history at any time to ensure you've taken your medications correctly. This feature is especially helpful for those with chronic conditions or those who need to manage multiple medications.

Using Emergency SOS and Medical ID

iOS offers important health and safety features designed to provide assistance in emergency situations. **Emergency SOS** and **Medical ID** are two features that can be life-saving, especially for seniors, people with health conditions, or anyone in need of urgent medical attention.

Setting Up Emergency SOS

1. **Activating Emergency SOS**

    - **Emergency SOS** is a feature that allows you to quickly call emergency services when you're in

distress. To activate it, press and hold the **side button** and either the **volume button** (on iPhone models with Face ID) or just the **side button** (on iPhone models with a Home button) until the **Emergency SOS slider** appears.
- Once the slider is visible, you can drag it to call emergency services immediately. If you continue to hold the buttons, your iPhone will automatically dial emergency services for you, even if you haven't activated the slider.

2. **Sending Emergency Alerts**

- In addition to calling emergency services, **Emergency SOS** will send a text message to your emergency contacts, alerting them that you've called for help. You can add emergency contacts in **Settings > Emergency SOS** and enable

Auto Call to allow for automatic emergency calls.
- This feature is particularly useful if you're unable to speak or use your device due to injury or other reasons.

Setting Up Medical ID

1. **Creating Your Medical ID**

    - The **Medical ID** feature allows you to store critical health information, such as allergies, medical conditions, medications, and emergency contacts, on your device. To set it up, open **Health**, tap on your **profile icon**, then select **Medical ID**.
    - Here, you can add important details such as your **name**, **date of birth**, **blood type**, **allergies**, and any medical conditions. You can also list your **emergency contacts**, and add any additional health

information that could assist first responders in an emergency.
2. **Accessing Medical ID in Emergencies**

    o Medical ID is accessible from the **lock screen**, so emergency responders can view it even if your phone is locked. To access it, swipe up on the **lock screen** and tap **Emergency** in the bottom-left corner. Then tap **Medical ID** to view your information.
    o It's important to ensure that your emergency contacts and medical details are kept up-to-date for your safety.

Security and Privacy with iOS

One of the key advantages of using iOS devices, such as iPhones and iPads, is the robust security and privacy features built into the operating system. Apple places a strong emphasis on protecting user data and ensuring that personal information remains secure from unauthorized access. With a variety of tools, settings, and features at your disposal, you can maintain a high level of privacy and control over who accesses your device and what information is shared with apps and services.

Setting Up Face ID, Touch ID, or Passcodes

Security begins with how you unlock your device, and iOS offers multiple secure methods for authentication, including **Face ID**, **Touch ID**, and the traditional **Passcode**. These methods ensure that only authorized users can access your device and its data.

Face ID

1. **What is Face ID?**

    Face ID is Apple's advanced facial recognition technology, available on devices with a TrueDepth camera system (like iPhone X and newer models). It scans your face to authenticate and unlock your device, as well as authorize payments and other secure actions.

2. **Setting Up Face ID**

    To set up **Face ID**, follow these steps:

    - Go to **Settings** > **Face ID & Passcode**.
    - Enter your **Passcode** to proceed.

- Tap **Set Up Face ID** and follow the on-screen instructions. You will be asked to position your face in front of the device's camera, and it will scan your face from different angles.
- Once Face ID is set up, you can enable or disable the options to use it for unlocking your iPhone, making payments with Apple Pay, or using third-party apps that support Face ID.

3. **Face ID Features**

   - Face ID is designed to work even with hats, glasses, and other accessories, but it's important to position your device at the correct distance from your face for optimal accuracy.
   - You can register multiple faces if you want to allow family members or trusted individuals access to your device.

- In **Settings > Face ID & Passcode**, you can also choose to enable or disable **Attention Aware Features**, which adjusts screen brightness and notifications based on whether you are looking at your phone.

Touch ID

1. **What is Touch ID?**

   Touch ID is Apple's fingerprint recognition system, available on devices with a **Home button** (iPhone 8 and earlier models) and some iPads. It uses a high-resolution scanner to read and store your fingerprint, providing a fast and secure way to unlock your device.

2. **Setting Up Touch ID**

   - Go to **Settings > Touch ID & Passcode** and enter your passcode.
   - Tap **Add a Fingerprint** and follow the instructions to place your finger on the Home button. It will scan

your fingerprint several times to ensure it captures all the necessary details for an accurate match.
  - Once set up, you can use Touch ID to unlock your device, make Apple Pay purchases, and authenticate other actions.
3. **Touch ID Features**

  - Touch ID is fast and secure, as it uses an encrypted local database to store your fingerprint data, ensuring that no one can access it without your consent.
  - You can register up to five fingerprints for multiple users or different fingers, offering flexibility for different use cases.
  - If you're using **Apple Pay**, Touch ID can authenticate payments for a simple, secure transaction.

Passcodes

1. **Why Use a Passcode?**

   A **Passcode** is a secure, traditional way to lock and unlock your device. It can be a 4-digit or 6-digit numeric code, or a custom alphanumeric password for added security. The passcode is used as an alternative or backup to **Face ID** or **Touch ID**, especially if biometric authentication is unavailable.

2. **Setting Up a Passcode**

   - Go to **Settings > Face ID & Passcode** (or **Touch ID & Passcode**).
   - Tap **Turn Passcode On** and enter your chosen code. If you select a custom alphanumeric code, you can enter a longer or more complex password for additional protection.
   - You'll be prompted to re-enter the passcode for verification.

3. **Passcode Features**

- The **Passcode** acts as a backup if Face ID or Touch ID fails (e.g., if your face is not recognized or your finger is wet).
- You can also enable options such as **Erase Data**, which will wipe your device after 10 failed attempts to enter the passcode, providing extra protection in case your device is stolen or accessed by unauthorized individuals.

Managing App Permissions

With the introduction of **App Tracking Transparency** and more granular **Privacy settings** in iOS, Apple gives you complete control over which apps can access sensitive data such as location, camera, microphone, photos, and more. Managing app permissions is crucial to protecting your personal information.

Viewing and Managing App Permissions

1. **Location Services**

   Apps that require access to your location (such as maps or weather apps) must request your permission. You can manage this permission in **Settings > Privacy > Location Services**. Here, you can:

   - Turn off location services entirely for all apps.
   - Set location access for individual apps to **Never, While Using the App**, or **Always**.
   - Enable **Share My Location** if you want to share your location with specific contacts.

2. **Camera and Microphone Access**

   iOS allows you to manage access to the **camera** and **microphone** for each app. To adjust these settings, go to **Settings > Privacy > Camera** and **Settings > Privacy > Microphone**. For example:

   - You can grant or deny camera access to apps like social media

platforms or video conferencing tools.
- Similarly, you can restrict microphone access to prevent apps from recording audio without your consent.

3. **Photos and Contacts**

    iOS gives you the option to allow apps to access your **Photos** and **Contacts**. You can either give apps **Read Only** access or provide them with full access to all your photos or contacts. For more control, iOS lets you grant access to only specific photos by selecting them from your photo library.

4. **Health Data Access**

    If you're using apps that collect or monitor health data, you can choose which data they can access. Go to **Settings > Privacy > Health** to manage which apps are allowed to read and write data to the **Health app**.

5. **App Privacy Report**
   With iOS 15 and later, you can view an **App Privacy Report** to see how your apps are using your data. This feature shows you which apps have accessed your location, photos, microphone, and other sensitive data within the past seven days. To enable this feature, go to **Settings > Privacy > App Privacy Report**.

Using Private Relay and Hide My Email

Apple offers some advanced privacy features to keep your browsing activities private and protect your identity when signing up for online services. These tools are part of Apple's broader initiative to enhance privacy for users, especially when interacting with websites and services that collect personal information.

Private Relay

1. **What is Private Relay?**

    Private Relay is a feature designed to protect your internet traffic from being tracked by third parties while browsing the web. It encrypts your browsing data and hides your IP address to prevent websites, advertisers, and other entities from tracking your online activities. This feature is available to **iCloud+** subscribers.

2. **How Private Relay Works**

    When you enable **Private Relay**, your internet traffic is routed through two separate relays:

    - The first relay sends the request for the website you want to visit, but it hides your IP address.
    - The second relay decrypts the information, allowing the website to know your region and provide localized content, but it doesn't

reveal your full IP address or personal data.
3. This process ensures that both your location and identity are protected from trackers and hackers.

4. **Enabling Private Relay**

    o To turn on **Private Relay**, go to **Settings > Your Name > iCloud > Private Relay**.
    o Toggle the switch to enable it. If you're using a network that may not support this feature (e.g., certain public Wi-Fi networks), you may see an option to disable it temporarily.

Hide My Email

1. **What is Hide My Email?**
   Hide My Email is another iCloud+ feature that allows you to create random, unique email addresses when signing up for services or making purchases online.

These temporary email addresses forward messages to your real email inbox but protect your identity and prevent your real email address from being shared or exposed.

2. **Using Hide My Email**

    - To use **Hide My Email**, go to **Settings > Your Name > iCloud > Hide My Email**. You can generate a random email address by tapping **Create new address**.
    - You can also use this feature directly when signing up for services or filling out forms on your device. iOS will suggest generating a **Hide My Email** address during the sign-up process.

3. **Managing Hide My Email Addresses**
    You can review, manage, and delete these temporary email addresses from the **Hide My Email** section in **iCloud settings**. This gives you complete control over the

unique email addresses created for each service.

Troubleshooting and Maintenance with iOS

Maintaining your iOS device's performance and resolving any technical issues that arise are essential parts of ensuring your device remains functional and reliable over time. Whether you're dealing with minor glitches, performance slowdowns, or just need help troubleshooting an issue, iOS offers a range of tools and procedures to keep things running smoothly.

Restarting, Updating, and Resetting Your Device

To keep your device running at its best, it's important to regularly restart it, update your iOS software, and reset your settings when necessary. These tasks can fix many common issues, improve performance, and provide solutions for malfunctioning apps or system errors.

Restarting Your Device

1. **Why Restarting Matters**
   Restarting your iPhone or iPad is one of the simplest yet effective ways to fix many minor issues. A restart clears the device's temporary cache, refreshes background processes, and resolves glitches such as unresponsive apps, slow performance, or connection issues.

2. **How to Restart Your iPhone or iPad**

   o **For iPhones with Face ID (iPhone X and later)**: Press and hold the **side button** and **volume up** or **volume down** button until the **Power off** slider appears. Slide to

power off the device, then press and hold the **side button** again to turn it back on.
- **For iPhones with a Home button (iPhone 8 and earlier)**: Press and hold the **top** (or **side**) button until the **Power off** slider appears. Slide to power off, and then hold the same button again to turn it back on.
3. **For iPads**: The process is similar to the iPhone. Press and hold the **top button** and **volume button** until the **Power off** slider appears, then slide to turn off the device. Turn it back on by holding the **top button**.

Updating Your Device

1. **Why Software Updates Are Important**
Software updates for iOS not only bring new features but also improve security and fix bugs or performance issues. Keeping your device updated ensures you benefit from the latest enhancements and

fixes for any existing problems.

2. **How to Update iOS**

    o Go to **Settings > General > Software Update**.
    o If an update is available, tap **Download and Install**. Your device will download the update and prompt you to install it once complete.
    o If you're on Wi-Fi and plugged into a charger, you can allow the update to install overnight.

3. **Automatic Updates**
   You can set your device to update automatically by going to **Settings > General > Software Update > Automatic Updates**. Enable **Download iOS Updates** and **Install iOS Updates** to ensure your device automatically installs updates when available.

Resetting Your Device

1. **When to Reset Your Device**

   If your device is consistently malfunctioning or experiencing major issues, a reset can restore it to factory settings. Resetting may be necessary when you encounter problems such as unresponsive apps, freezing, or a slow performance that can't be fixed by other methods.

2. **How to Perform a Soft Reset**

   A **soft reset** (reboot) can help resolve minor issues without affecting your data. It's the same as restarting your device, as described earlier.

3. **Hard Reset (Factory Reset)**

   - To erase all data and reset your device to factory settings, go to **Settings > General > Reset**, then

choose **Erase All Content and Settings**.
- **Warning**: This will remove all your data, including apps, photos, and settings. Be sure to back up your device to **iCloud** or **iTunes** before performing a factory reset.
4. **Reset Network Settings**
If you're having trouble with Wi-Fi, Bluetooth, or cellular connections, resetting network settings might solve the issue. Go to **Settings > General > Reset > Reset Network Settings**. This will reset Wi-Fi networks, passwords, and cellular settings but won't affect your data.

Managing Storage and Backups with iCloud

Maintaining adequate storage and regular backups is crucial for the longevity and safety of your device. If you're running low on storage or concerned about losing important data, managing your storage and backing up regularly are key steps to keep your device running smoothly.

Managing Storage on iOS

1. **Check Storage Usage**
    - Go to **Settings** > **General** > **iPhone Storage** (or **iPad Storage**). This screen shows a breakdown of storage usage by apps, photos, videos, and system data. You'll be able to see which apps are using the most space and make decisions on what to delete or offload.
2. **Freeing Up Storage**
    - **Offload Unused Apps**: iOS offers an option to **offload unused apps** automatically. This removes the app but keeps its data, allowing you to reinstall it without losing any information.
    - **Clear Cache**: Some apps, especially browsers and social media apps, accumulate cache over

time. You can clear these caches within individual app settings (like Safari's cache under **Settings > Safari > Clear History and Website Data**).
- **Delete Old Photos and Videos**: Large media files often take up a lot of storage. Consider using **iCloud Photos** to back up your photos and videos and delete those you no longer need.
- **Delete or Offload Large Files**: In **iPhone Storage**, check for large files, like videos, that can be deleted or moved to **iCloud Drive**.

Using iCloud for Backups

1. **Why Use iCloud Backup?**
 iCloud ensures that all your important data, such as photos, contacts, apps, and settings, are automatically backed up in case your device is lost, stolen, or needs a reset.

2. **Setting Up iCloud Backup**

    - Go to **Settings > [Your Name] > iCloud > iCloud Backup**.
    - Toggle the switch to **On**. Your device will automatically back up to iCloud when connected to Wi-Fi, plugged into a charger, and the screen is locked.
    - You can tap **Back Up Now** to manually trigger an immediate backup.

3. **Restoring from iCloud Backup**

    - If you need to restore from an iCloud backup (such as after a factory reset), during the setup process on a new device or after a reset, select **Restore from iCloud Backup** and sign in with your Apple ID. Choose the most recent backup and wait for your device to restore all your data.

4. **Managing iCloud Storage**

    o If you're running low on iCloud storage, you can manage it by going to **Settings > [Your Name] > iCloud > Manage Storage**. You can delete old backups, manage app data, or purchase more iCloud storage if necessary.

Common Issues and How to Fix Them

iPhones and iPads are generally reliable, but occasional issues can arise. Below are some common problems and simple troubleshooting steps you can follow to fix them.

1. iPhone Not Turning On

- **Cause**: A frozen system or drained battery could prevent your iPhone from turning on.
- **Fix**:

- Plug your device into a charger and wait for a few minutes. If the battery was drained, it may need a few minutes before the screen turns on.
- Perform a **hard reset** (force restart) by pressing and releasing the **Volume Up** button, then the **Volume Down** button, followed by holding the **Side** button until the Apple logo appears.

2. Apps Freezing or Crashing

- **Cause**: Apps may freeze or crash due to bugs, lack of storage, or outdated versions.
- **Fix**:
  - Close the app and reopen it. Double-click the Home button or swipe up from the bottom to access the app switcher, then swipe up on the app to close it.

- If the issue persists, try restarting your device or updating the app via the **App Store**.
- If that doesn't work, try deleting the app and reinstalling it.

3. Wi-Fi or Bluetooth Connectivity Issues

- **Cause**: Connectivity problems can arise due to software issues, network problems, or misconfigured settings.
- **Fix**:
    - Restart your device and the router or modem.
    - Toggle **Wi-Fi** and **Bluetooth** off and on via **Control Center** or in the **Settings** app.
    - Reset network settings under **Settings > General > Reset > Reset Network Settings**.
    - Ensure that your device is within range of the Wi-Fi network or Bluetooth device.

4. Battery Draining Quickly

- **Cause**: Battery drain can occur due to background app refresh, location services, or battery-hungry apps.
- **Fix**:
    - Go to **Settings > Battery** to see which apps are using the most battery.
    - Disable **Background App Refresh** for apps that don't need it by going to **Settings > General > Background App Refresh**.
    - Adjust **Location Services** and disable unnecessary location tracking in **Settings > Privacy > Location Services**.

5. Slow Performance

- **Cause**: Overloaded storage, outdated software, or too many background apps can slow down performance.
- **Fix**:
    - Clear storage by offloading apps, deleting old photos and videos, and clearing browser caches.

- Update to the latest version of iOS.
- Restart your device to free up memory and resources.

Advanced Tips and Tricks for iOS 18.2

While iOS offers a user-friendly experience, it also has a wealth of advanced features that can make your device even more powerful, personalized, and efficient. Whether you're looking to make your daily tasks easier with Siri and automation or connect your iPhone or iPad to other Apple devices, mastering these advanced tips and tricks will help you unlock the full potential of iOS 18.2.

Using Siri for Voice Commands and Automation

Siri is Apple's voice assistant that helps you complete tasks hands-free, making it easier to interact with your device without needing to touch the screen. Beyond simple voice commands, Siri's capabilities extend to powerful automation features that can make your life easier.

1. Voice Commands with Siri

Siri's primary function is responding to voice commands to help you with a wide range of tasks. By activating Siri, you can execute numerous commands that save time and make navigating iOS much more convenient.

How to Use Siri:
 You can activate Siri in several ways depending on your device:

- **iPhones with Face ID**: Say "Hey Siri" or press and hold the **side button**.
- **iPhones with a Home button**: Press and hold the **Home button**.
- **iPads**: Use the same method as iPhones.

Once activated, you can issue commands like:

- "Send a message to [contact name]."
- "Play music from [artist name]."
- "Set an alarm for 7 a.m."
- "What's the weather like today?"
- "Turn on Wi-Fi."

Siri can also answer questions, set reminders, provide directions, make phone calls, and send texts—all hands-free, making it an invaluable tool for busy users.

2. Siri for Automation: Siri Shortcuts

One of the most powerful features of Siri is its integration with **Shortcuts**, allowing users to automate multiple steps in a process using a single voice command. Shortcuts can range from simple tasks like turning on Do Not Disturb and starting a playlist to complex routines such as adjusting your home's smart thermostat, controlling lights, and opening apps in a specific sequence.

Creating and Managing Shortcuts:

To create a custom Siri Shortcut, follow these steps:

- Open the **Shortcuts** app on your iPhone or iPad.
- Tap the + icon in the top right corner to create a new shortcut.
- Tap **Add Action** to choose an action you want to automate (e.g., sending a message, playing music, controlling smart home devices).
- After adding actions, you can combine them in a sequence to automate a complete process.
- Tap **Next**, name your shortcut, and then tap **Add to Siri** to record a custom voice command for it.

Once your Shortcut is created, you can trigger it by saying the designated phrase, such as:

- "Hey Siri, start my morning routine."
- "Hey Siri, I'm home."

With iOS 18.2, Apple continues to improve the Shortcuts app, allowing for deeper integration with more apps, custom automations based on specific triggers, and more advanced scripting capabilities.

3. Siri and Personal Automation:

iOS 18.2 includes enhancements to **Personal Automations** in the Shortcuts app. This allows your device to trigger actions automatically based on specific events, like:

- **Time of day** (e.g., turning on your favorite playlist at a specific time).
- **Location** (e.g., turning off Wi-Fi when leaving home).
- **App launches** (e.g., turning on Focus mode when opening work-related apps).
- **Bluetooth connections** (e.g., automatically playing music when connecting to your car's Bluetooth).

To create an automation, open the **Shortcuts** app and select the **Automation** tab. From there, you can choose from a variety of triggers, customize the actions, and schedule them to run based on specific conditions.

Creating and Managing Shortcuts

Shortcuts can significantly increase your productivity by reducing the number of steps required to complete daily tasks. Here's a deeper dive into how to create, manage, and organize shortcuts effectively.

1. Finding Pre-made Shortcuts

Apple provides a library of pre-made shortcuts that are simple to add and use. You can browse them in the **Gallery** section of the **Shortcuts** app. These shortcuts are divided into categories such as **Morning Routine**, **Music**, **Home**, and **Productivity**, making it easy to find ones that match your needs.

- To add a pre-made shortcut, tap on it in the **Gallery** and then hit **Add Shortcut** to add it to your library.

2. Customizing Shortcuts

You can customize each shortcut to perform specific actions that suit your personal or professional needs. To edit an existing shortcut, simply tap on it in the **My Shortcuts** tab, and you can add, delete, or rearrange actions. Shortcuts can include:

- **App actions**: Open apps, send messages, post to social media.
- **Media actions**: Play music, adjust volume, create photos.
- **Web actions**: Search the web, download files, or use URLs.
- **Smart home actions**: Control lights, locks, or thermostats using HomeKit.

3. Organizing Shortcuts

As you create more shortcuts, it's important to keep them organized for easy access. You can organize them into folders in the **My Shortcuts** section of the app. Simply tap **Select**, then choose the shortcuts you want to group together and tap **Add to Folder**.

4. Using Shortcuts Widgets

For quick access, you can add your favorite shortcuts as widgets on the Home Screen or Lock Screen. To do so, tap and hold on the Home Screen, enter **Jiggle Mode**, and tap the + button to add a **Shortcuts** widget. From there, you can choose individual shortcuts or sets of shortcuts to display.

Connecting to Other Apple Devices

One of the greatest advantages of iOS is its seamless integration with other Apple products. Whether you have an Apple Watch, Mac, Apple TV, or AirPods, iOS offers numerous ways to connect your devices and enhance your experience.

1. Continuity and Handoff

iOS devices support **Continuity**, which allows you to start an activity on one Apple device and seamlessly continue it on another. Some examples of Continuity features include:

- **Handoff**: Start reading an email on your iPhone, and pick up where you left off on your Mac or iPad. The same applies to apps like Safari, Notes, Maps, and Messages.
- **Universal Clipboard**: Copy something (text, image, or link) on your iPhone and paste it onto your Mac or iPad.
- **AirDrop**: Transfer files, photos, or documents wirelessly between Apple devices. To use AirDrop, select the file or content you wish to share, tap the **Share** icon, and choose the target device from the AirDrop options.

2. Apple Watch and iPhone Integration

If you have an Apple Watch, your iPhone works seamlessly with it to offer extended functionality. You can:

- Receive and respond to messages, calls, and notifications directly from your wrist.
- Use your watch to track health and fitness metrics, which syncs directly with your iPhone.
- Unlock your Mac with the Apple Watch using **Auto Unlock**.
- Control media, play music, or adjust volume using the **Now Playing** app.

3. Connecting to Apple TV

With iOS 18.2, the ability to control and interact with your Apple TV has been improved. You can use your iPhone as a remote control for your Apple TV through the **Apple TV Remote** function in the **Control Center**.

- Access the remote by swiping down from the top-right corner of your iPhone screen

and tapping on the **Apple TV Remote** icon.
- You can also share content from your iPhone to Apple TV using **AirPlay** to stream photos, videos, and music.

4. AirPods and iPhone

AirPods provide a seamless audio experience when connected to your iPhone. Features include:

- **Automatic Switching**: AirPods automatically switch between Apple devices, such as from your iPhone to your Mac, based on which device is playing audio.
- **Spatial Audio**: Enhanced sound experience with dynamic head-tracking when using supported apps on iOS 18.2.
- **Siri Integration**: Ask Siri to play music, set reminders, or make calls directly through your AirPods.

5. iCloud Integration Across Devices

iOS 18.2 Bible

iCloud allows you to keep your data synced across all your Apple devices, including contacts, calendars, photos, documents, and more. By enabling iCloud, you ensure that your data is always up-to-date and accessible, whether you're on your iPhone, iPad, or Mac.

iOS 18.2 Hidden Gems

iOS is a dynamic operating system, constantly evolving with new features, enhancements, and surprises that can sometimes go unnoticed by the average user. iOS 18.2, with its array of refinements and tools, offers a rich set of features that can significantly enhance the iPhone and iPad experience.

Discovering New Features in iOS 18.2

Each iOS release brings new functionality and refinements, and iOS 18.2 is no exception. While some of the features are highly publicized, others are tucked away in settings or hidden within specific apps, waiting to be discovered.

1. Enhanced Widgets Customization

Widgets on iOS have become more customizable than ever in iOS 18.2. Apple has expanded the ability to add, remove, and customize widgets on the Home Screen, allowing users to tailor their device to suit their preferences. Here's how to make the most of it:

- **Interactive Widgets**: Many widgets are now interactive, meaning you can take actions directly from the widget itself without having to open the app. For example, in the **Weather** widget, you can toggle between forecasts for different locations, while the **Music** widget lets you pause or play music directly.
- **Stacked Widgets**: You can stack multiple widgets on top of each other and swipe through them easily. To stack widgets, simply drag one widget on top of another on the Home Screen. This is especially

useful for users who prefer minimalism but still want quick access to information.

2. Live Activities in More Apps

In iOS 18.2, the **Live Activities** feature—first introduced in iOS 16—has been expanded to more apps, providing real-time updates for ongoing events like sports games, delivery tracking, or flight statuses.

- **Example**: When ordering food through a third-party app, you can track the status of your delivery in real-time directly from the Lock Screen or Dynamic Island (for iPhone models with this feature).
- **How to Enable**: Many apps automatically support Live Activities, but you can also find them by checking out **Settings > Notifications** and ensuring **Live Activities** are enabled for supported apps.

3. Focus Mode Enhancements

Focus modes, which were first introduced in iOS 15, continue to evolve, with iOS 18.2 bringing more powerful ways to customize your device's behavior based on what you're doing.

- **Focus Filters**: iOS 18.2 allows you to create specific **Focus Filters**, which customize app behaviors and settings within a particular focus. For example, you can silence specific notifications, filter out certain websites from Safari, or even limit certain app features when you're in "Work Mode" or "Personal Mode."
- **Focus Mode Customization**: More apps now support Focus Mode, including customizable Home Screen layouts for each mode. You can create a Home Screen specifically for work or relaxation, and your apps will change automatically depending on the Focus you've selected.

4. Advanced Security Features for Privacy

Apple continues to prioritize user privacy, and iOS 18.2 introduces new tools for managing your data securely.

- **App Privacy Report**: This tool, found under **Settings > Privacy > App Privacy Report**, provides transparency on how apps are using your data, including what data they're collecting, what websites they're tracking you across, and how often they access sensitive information like your camera or microphone.
- **Hide My Email Enhancements**: With **Hide My Email**, you can generate random email addresses to protect your real one. In iOS 18.2, this tool is further integrated with third-party apps, providing a layer of privacy while signing up for services.

5. Enhanced CarPlay Experience

CarPlay, Apple's in-car system, has received some cool updates in iOS 18.2, making it more useful for everyday drivers.

- **New App Categories**: iOS 18.2 introduces new categories for navigation, music, and climate control. You can now

access the most relevant apps more easily, making your driving experience smoother.
- **Home Screen Customization**: Just like with your device's Home Screen, CarPlay's layout can now be customized, with options to add widgets, change app placement, and even organize different sections of the screen.

Tips for Power Users

For those who are comfortable with iOS and want to take things to the next level, iOS 18.2 offers several advanced features that can streamline workflows, enhance multitasking, and further personalize the experience.

1. Multitasking with Stage Manager (for iPad Pro)

For iPad Pro users, iOS 18.2 introduces **Stage Manager**, an enhanced multitasking feature that offers a more desktop-like experience, allowing users to run multiple apps in a floating window format.

- **How to Use**: To activate Stage Manager, swipe down from the top-left corner of the screen (or swipe up with four fingers), and apps will appear as resizable windows. You can switch between windows, overlap them, and organize your workspace.

2. Automating Tasks with Advanced Shortcuts

The **Shortcuts** app is one of the most powerful tools for power users, as it lets you automate virtually any aspect of your device. In iOS 18.2, Shortcuts has become even more robust, allowing users to:

- Create **multi-step automations**: Combine actions such as launching apps, adjusting settings, and sending messages with one command.

- Use **Focus Mode triggers**: Automatically change your Focus settings when opening certain apps or reaching specific locations.
- **Advanced scripting**: Use the **Run JavaScript** action to integrate custom scripts and add even more complex functions to your shortcuts.

3. App Clips for Quick Interactions

App Clips allow you to use small parts of an app without fully installing it. iOS 18.2 enhances this feature by integrating App Clips into more scenarios.

- **How to Use**: App Clips are available by scanning QR codes or tapping NFC tags in real-world locations, like restaurants or public transport stations. You can pay for goods, check-in to events, or access information instantly—without needing to download the full app.

4. Command Center Customization

For power users who want instant access to key features, iOS 18.2 offers expanded **Control Center** options. You can now add shortcuts for more system functions, such as:

- **Live Activities**: Quickly access Live Activities directly from the Control Center.
- **Focus Mode**: Toggle between different Focus modes without having to navigate through multiple settings.
- **QR Code Scanner**: Add a quick access shortcut for scanning QR codes.

5. Screen Time Customizations for Advanced Control

For users who want complete control over their device's usage and content, iOS 18.2 allows advanced customizations within **Screen Time**. You can now:

- **Create custom downtime schedules** based on different days of the week.

- Set **app limits** not just for specific apps, but for app categories, including games, social media, or productivity apps.
- **App Usage Reports**: Go beyond the basic reports and view detailed breakdowns of app usage patterns, including specific times of day and activities.

Upcoming Features in Future Updates

While iOS 18.2 brings several powerful features, Apple is continuously working on new updates that will refine the operating system even further. Here are some of the most anticipated features expected in future iOS releases:

1. Enhanced Augmented Reality (AR) Capabilities

Apple has been investing heavily in AR, and future iOS updates are likely to expand its capabilities further. New tools may be introduced to support the development of more interactive AR experiences across apps, games, and navigation.

2. Pro Mode for Power Users

Some rumors suggest Apple is planning to introduce a **Pro Mode**, designed for users who need enhanced system performance. Pro Mode would allow users to fine-tune their iPhone or iPad's performance settings, prioritizing speed and responsiveness for demanding tasks such as gaming, video editing, or multitasking.

3. Health and Fitness Expansion

Apple continues to prioritize health and wellness, and future iOS updates will likely enhance the **Health app** with more data integration, such as tracking more vital signs (e.g., blood sugar or sleep apnea) and deeper integration with third-party devices and services.

4. More Focused Smart Home Integration

Apple is expected to improve the integration of **HomeKit** with iOS in upcoming releases, making smart home control more intuitive, reliable, and capable of handling more complex automations.

5. iCloud Improvements

Expect iCloud to expand with more seamless cross-platform syncing, possibly including additional storage features, such as faster backup speeds and more control over backup settings across devices.

Appendices

The following appendices provide additional resources, terminology explanations, and tips to help you maximize your understanding of iOS 18.2. Whether you are a beginner or a power user, these appendices offer essential tools and references to enhance your experience with iOS.

Glossary of iOS Terms

Understanding iOS terminology is essential for navigating the operating system and utilizing its features effectively. Here is a comprehensive glossary of key terms commonly used in iOS, including some specific to iOS 18.2.

1. Apple ID
 Your Apple ID is your personal account used to

access Apple services like the App Store, iCloud, Apple Music, and more. It allows synchronization of your data across all Apple devices and facilitates purchases and subscriptions.

2. App Clips
 Small parts of apps that you can use without downloading the full app. App Clips are designed for quick, specific interactions such as paying for goods or accessing a specific service.

3. App Store
 Apple's digital storefront for downloading apps, games, and other content for iOS devices. The App Store is where you'll find most apps for productivity, entertainment, education, and much more.

4. Control Center
 A panel that provides quick access to essential system controls like Wi-Fi, Bluetooth, Do Not Disturb, and brightness. It can be accessed by swiping down from the top-right corner (for

Face ID devices) or up from the bottom (for Touch ID devices).

5. Dynamic Island

A new feature on iPhone models with a notch (starting with the iPhone 14 Pro), Dynamic Island is an interactive area that provides live information and notifications for things like calls, music playback, or timers.

6. Face ID

Apple's facial recognition system used for unlocking your iPhone, making payments, and accessing sensitive apps or information securely. It uses sensors and a front-facing camera to map and recognize your face.

7. Focus Mode

A feature that allows you to customize your notifications and Home Screen depending on your current activity. You can set up different Focus Modes for work, personal time, driving, etc.

8. iCloud

Apple's cloud-based storage service that allows you to back up and sync your data, such as photos, contacts, calendars, and documents, across all Apple devices.

9. iMessage

Apple's proprietary messaging service that allows users to send text messages, images, videos, and audio messages over the internet instead of using SMS/MMS. It works exclusively between Apple devices.

10. Live Activities

Real-time updates displayed on the Lock Screen or Dynamic Island, such as sports scores, delivery status, or workout progress, that keep you informed without needing to open the app.

11. Lock Screen

The screen that appears when you wake your device, where you can view notifications, access widgets, and quickly unlock your phone using Face ID, Touch ID, or a passcode.

12. Multitasking

The ability to run multiple apps simultaneously. In iOS 18.2, this includes new multitasking features for iPad, such as **Stage Manager**, which allows you to open multiple apps in resizable windows for a desktop-like experience.

13. Notification Center

The panel that shows your notifications, such as messages, app alerts, and reminders. It can be accessed by swiping down from the top of the screen (on devices with Face ID) or from the top-center (on devices with Touch ID).

14. Siri

Apple's virtual assistant that can perform tasks like setting reminders, sending messages, making phone calls, and answering questions. Siri can be activated via voice or the device's side button.

15. Spotlight Search

A search tool that helps you find apps, documents, emails, messages, web results, and even perform calculations directly from your device's Home Screen.

16. Stage Manager
A feature on iPadOS that allows users to manage multiple apps in floating windows, making it easier to multitask. This feature is available on iPads with M1 chips and later.

17. Widgets
Small app extensions that display useful information on the Home Screen or Lock Screen, such as weather, calendar events, or news updates. Widgets in iOS 18.2 can now be more interactive and customizable.

18. iOS
Apple's operating system for iPhone and iPad, which provides the interface, features, and functionality for managing apps, settings, notifications, and more.

Keyboard Shortcuts for iPad and iPhone

iOS devices, particularly iPads, come with a variety of keyboard shortcuts that can help users perform tasks faster and more efficiently. Whether you're using a Bluetooth keyboard, the iPad's Smart Keyboard, or the on-screen keyboard, these shortcuts are great tools for power users.

General Shortcuts for iPhone and iPad

- **Home Screen**:
    - **Cmd + Space**: Open Spotlight Search.
    - **Cmd + H**: Go to the Home Screen.
    - **Cmd + Shift + 3**: Take a screenshot.
    - **Cmd + Shift + 4**: Capture a screenshot of the selected area.
- **App Navigation**:
    - **Cmd + Tab**: Switch between recently used apps.
    - **Cmd + Q**: Close the current app (works with certain apps).
    - **Cmd + W**: Close the current window (for apps like Safari).

- **Cmd + R**: Reload the page (in Safari).
- **Text Editing**:
    - **Cmd + C**: Copy selected text.
    - **Cmd + V**: Paste copied text.
    - **Cmd + X**: Cut selected text.
    - **Cmd + A**: Select all text.
    - **Cmd + Z**: Undo the previous action.
    - **Cmd + Shift + Z**: Redo the previous action.
- **Safari Shortcuts**:
    - **Cmd + T**: Open a new tab.
    - **Cmd + L**: Highlight the URL bar.
    - **Cmd + N**: Open a new window.
    - **Cmd + D**: Add current page to bookmarks.

Shortcuts for iPad with External Keyboard

- **Multitasking**:
    - **Cmd + Option + D**: Show or hide the Dock.

- **Cmd + Option + Left/Right Arrow**: Switch between Slide Over apps.
  - **Cmd + Option + Space**: Show the App Switcher.
  - **Cmd + Option + M**: Minimize the current app.
- **App Switching**:
  - **Cmd + Tab**: Switch between open apps.
  - **Cmd + Shift + Tab**: Switch to the previous app.
  - **Cmd + 1-9**: Switch between open apps (in the Dock).

Text Shortcuts

- **Cmd + B**: Bold text.
- **Cmd + I**: Italicize text.
- **Cmd + U**: Underline text.
- **Cmd + K**: Insert a hyperlink (in compatible apps like Mail and Safari).

Special iPad Shortcuts

- **Cmd + Option + M**: Minimize all apps (return to Home Screen).
- **Cmd + Shift + H**: Access the Home Screen.
- **Cmd + Shift + L**: Lock your iPad.

These keyboard shortcuts are particularly useful for iPad users who are working with an external keyboard, helping to streamline multitasking and increase productivity.

Resources for Learning More

To help deepen your understanding of iOS 18.2 and continue learning, here are some valuable resources for users of all experience levels.

1. Apple Support Website

- **URL**: https://support.apple.com/
  The official Apple Support website is the most comprehensive resource for troubleshooting, learning about iOS features, and finding solutions to common

issues. You can access articles, how-to guides, troubleshooting tips, and more.

2. Apple Community Forums

- **URL**: https://discussions.apple.com/
 Apple's Community Forums are an excellent place to ask questions, share experiences, and get advice from other users. Whether you're troubleshooting an issue or looking for tips, the forums are a great place to connect with other iOS users.

3. iOS User Guide

- **URL**: https://support.apple.com/guide/iphone/welcome/ios
 The iOS User Guide provides detailed, step-by-step instructions on using all iOS features. It covers everything from basic functions to advanced tips and can be accessed for free online or via the Apple Books app.

4. iOS 18.2 Release Notes

- **URL**: https://www.apple.com/ios/ios-18/
  Release notes detail all the new features, enhancements, and fixes that come with the latest iOS updates. For users wanting to stay up-to-date with every iOS release, reading the official release notes is key.

5. YouTube Channels

Several YouTube channels provide excellent iOS tutorials, reviews, and tips. Some popular channels include:

- **Apple Support**: Apple's official channel offers a variety of instructional videos.
- **iDeviceHelp**: This channel provides in-depth tutorials and tips on iPhone, iPad, and iOS.
- **MacRumors**: Great for news, rumors, and in-depth iOS feature reviews.

6. Online Courses and Tutorials

- **Udemy**: Offers several iOS courses that cover everything from basic iPhone usage to app development for iOS.
- **Skillshare**: A great platform for creative professionals, offering courses on using iOS apps for productivity, video editing, and more.

7. Books

- **"iPhone: The Missing Manual"** by David Pogue
  A comprehensive guide to iOS devices, this book covers everything from setup to advanced features.
- **"iOS 18 For Dummies"** by John Wiley & Sons
  A beginner-friendly guide that breaks down iOS 18.2 features and how to use them in an accessible way.

iOS 18.2 Bible

Made in United States
Orlando, FL
01 January 2025